MW01493326

The APOSTOLIC
Mandate

Book 1 - The Apostolic Field Guide Series

COLETTE TOACH

www.ami-bookshop.com

The Apostolic Mandate
Book 1 - The Apostolic Field Guide Series

ISBN-10: 1-62664-173-0
ISBN-13: 978-1-62664-173-0

Copyright © **2017** by Apostolic Movement International, LLC.
All rights reserved
5663 Balboa Ave #416,
San Diego,
California 92111,
United States of America

1ˢᵗ Printing September 2017

Published by **Apostolic Movement International, LLC**
E-mail Address: admin@ami-bookshop.com
Web Address: www.ami-bookshop.com

Unless specified, all Scripture references taken from the New King James Version®.
Copyright © 1982 by Thomas Nelson. Used by permission. All rights reserved.

CONTENTS

10 DECEMBER 1974

CHAPTER 01 – 10 DECEMBER 1974

If you know a little bit of history, you know that this date means absolutely nothing to the rest of the world. It only means something to me because it is my date of birth. It's the day that I was the first born to the Crause family.

My father rushed to the hospital. He just missed the birth. He arrived and ran straight into the nurse who had this screaming bundle in her arms on the way to be washed.

She said, "Oh, you are the father?"

Then, they dumped me into his hands.

Here is this poor, 22-year-old new dad, not knowing what he is going to do with this child. He held me, looked down at me, and got the fright of his life. He looked into my face and saw himself looking back at him.

I was a spitting image of him. Right there, before I even had my first bath, he held me up to the Lord. He dedicated me for the work of God.

My father came from a line of preachers. He grew up in a home where his parents were involved in ministry. He knew what it was like to be a pastor's kid.

I have one up on him. I grew up as an apostle's kid.

That is no walk in the park. If he was different, I was even more different. If he was an outcast, I was an even greater outcast.

From the day that I took my first breath, God had a plan for my life.

> **Galatians 1:15** *But when it pleased God, who separated me from my mother's womb and called me through His grace.*

> *Whether a man or a woman, when you are called
> for such a walk in the Lord, it is by His grace.*

It is not based on what you have accomplished, done or how great you are. It is not even about how many skills you have. It is simply by His grace.

CHILDHOOD — TRAINING IN THE HOME

I grew up in a home where we were actively involved in ministry. I tried to think back on a time in my life where we were not in some ministry, church, or meeting. However, as far back as I can remember, we were involved in ministry.

As soon as I could understand the gifts of the Spirit, I was flowing in them. This was a very common thing in our home. We would have a prayer time, and we would share the visions and impressions that we felt the Lord was giving us.

It was also common to share dreams that I had with my father. He would help interpret them for me. He would say, "The Lord is telling you what is ahead of you."

I grew up in this. It was not a "super-duper" event to talk to the Lord, get revelation, or have new teachings.

There was only one desire that my father had for any of us. His desire was that we would serve the Lord. He did not put pressure on us to become great in the world or to get a great career.

He supported us in whatever we decided to do, even if we were off into rebellion. He knew that God was greater than anything else.

He just wanted us to serve God.

So, it never occurred to me that I would not serve God. I knew when the time came that I would rise up and serve Him.

You may find this strange, but it never occurred to me that I was a woman.

I grew up in a home with two sisters. We were taught to stand in the fullness of our femininity and be real women. However, we never had a turn of life event talk about how the reality is that "women and ministry do not mix".

My father skipped that whole "fact of life speech", and I was blissfully naïve concerning that. It never occurred to me that being a woman was a problem in ministry.

In my naivety, I went forward. Around the age of fourteen, I received my own call from the Lord.

AN ENCOUNTER WITH JESUS

You must realize that up until this time, I was the pastor's daughter. I had been playing the drums and been in the worship band. There was continual pressure because I was the pastor's daughter.

I was to be perfect and sinless. I was expected to know all the answers.

I was in active ministry, giving counsel, teaching, and involved in church leadership from the age of eleven. This was not anything unusual. It was the environment I was born into. I truly knew no different.

There came a time, however, when I thought, "Lord, I know that You have birthed me into this family, but do I have a say here about my call?"

"Am I just called because I was born into this family, or do I really have a calling?"

That is when I met the Lord Jesus for the first time at the age of fourteen.

I was in a transition phase where my mother had left. My father and I would spend long periods of time in intercession. During one of those times, I saw the Lord Jesus come near me on a white horse, dressed as a king.

At first, I did not realize who He was. I just saw this majestic king on His white horse. Then, He stepped down and took my hand. When I looked into His face, He said, "Follow me."

I knew that this was the Lord Jesus.

It was the first time that I had a personal face-to-face encounter with Him. That is when I received my call.

A couple of months later, everything went wrong. I went well off the rails, straight into rebellion. Satan attacked me from every angle. The needs and bitterness concerning my parent's divorce rose up inside of me. I had a hunger I could not satisfy. A bitterness that gnawed at my heart.

I could no longer live up to the grand expectations. I was wary of being perfect. I was frustrated of always being on the outside looking in. I hungered for normality, and my experience with Jesus faded into the background.

Thinking back on my experience with Him, I said to myself, "I clearly missed it. I do not know what I was thinking. Forget about this ministry thing. There's too much pressure and stress. I am out of here."

> *Ezekiel 16:9* *"Then I washed you in water; yes, I thoroughly washed off your blood, and I anointed you with oil.*
>
> *10 I clothed you in embroidered cloth and gave you sandals of badger skin; I clothed you with fine linen and covered you with silk.*
>
> *11 I adorned you with ornaments, put bracelets on your wrists, and a chain on your neck.*
>
> *12 And I put a jewel in your nose, earrings in your ears, and a beautiful crown on your head.*
>
> *13 Thus you were adorned with gold and silver, and your clothing was of fine linen, silk, and embroidered cloth. You ate pastry of fine flour, honey, and oil. You were exceedingly beautiful, and succeeded to royalty.*

I ran into the world, only to find Jesus waiting for me there. I ran and ran until He captured my heart in His hands and made this passage my personal renewal. The Lord looked at me while I was in my rebellion. He chased after me, picked me up, cleaned me off, and placed bracelets on my hand.

When I was feeling lost, He called me royalty. Feeling empty, He filled me with His grace. Knowing I had failed, He adored me with gold and silver. My greatest boast as to why I qualify to walk in this office? There is none.

Where did the Father find you? What pit did He draw you from? The mud pit of loneliness or the dungeons of rebellion?

HOW HE DID IT...

Jesus reached into the night clubs I was going to, and the waitress job I had settled into, and caught me with something that I could not resist. He introduced me to Craig. If it was not for my husband, I probably would not be writing this today.

The Lord was sneaky. He knew that if I was going to fulfill this mandate, I needed some extra pressure. I am an expressive after all. I needed a goal and a good reason. So, the Lord gave me a good reason.

I started dating this long-haired, scruffy, heavy metal, head banging, crazy guy. He was so opposite to everything that I was brought up to believe was "wholesome". I thought, "This is perfect!"

That was the case until we visited my parents one night. My father went and led him to the Lord.

Wait, there's even more. Craig got Spirit-filled, spoke in tongues, prophesied, and said, "Lord, use me for anything."

Imagine me standing there thinking, "Did anyone ask me if I wanted to get on this bus?"

If I was going to keep up with this new love of my life, I knew that I had some things to do.

Right there, my father put his hands on us, married us in the spirit, sealed us as a couple, and sealed us for the work of the ministry.

He said, "I see you on an airplane with two small children. You are being called to the nations."

This was a bit bigger than playing in the worship band. It sounded exciting. I thought, "Perhaps we will get married, get some careers, and then get going in about five to seven years."

I figured that we would ease into the children and the whole "flying across the world thing". However, just two and a half years later, Craig and I were on a plane bound for San Diego with our one and two-year-old daughters (Deborah-Anne and Jessica).

By then, the Lord had drawn me to Himself, and Craig was leading the way with his fire and newfound passion for the Lord Jesus. For the first year of our marriage, he was the one dragging me along and imparting to me the fire of what I had taken for granted my entire life.

Well, the whole idea that "we had time" was not to be.

When God moves, He does it quickly.

We joined my parents in the work of the ministry, and we got involved immediately.

One evening, we were having our usual prayer time as a team.

My father said, "Colette! I see this key for you in the spirit."

I thought, "Give it to me, Lord. I am here. I am ready."

My father said, "I do not know what this key means. It is a jewel encrusted key, and it looks important."

He prayed, prophesied, and released it.

The next day, I was dying! My flesh was exploding in a hundred directions, and "my righteousness" was tested!

After a week I said, "Was that the key of death?"

Everything went wrong. Every pressure that could, came at me from every side.

KEY OF DAVID

It was around that time that the Lord started to give him a revelation of the apostolic. What he had given me is called the key of David in the Scriptures.

We see it many times when we release an apostle into training. It is a very specific key for a very particular training. I do not wish it on my worst enemy. It is a very intense training.

I was still very naïve here, and I still did not marry the "woman and apostolic" thing together.

The Lord said, "I have given you this key."

I died and resurrected and died and resurrected. That was good enough for me.

It never occurred to me that being a woman and an apostle was a problem.

You did not need to tell me that something was happening. Most days, I had one foot in the grave and one out of the grave.

It was real. I could say, "On this day, I clearly was released into something."

It was fully by the hand of the Holy Spirit. Craig and I had some learning to do on our own. When we first got married, in that two-and-a-half-year period that I threw past you, I had no ministry involvement for a while.

In fact, my parents came to Mexico a year ahead of us. Craig and I were left alone for a year in South Africa.

BACKTRACK A LITTLE BIT...

Can you picture me joining a regular status quo church with my husband and children? That is what we did.

I needed to go there, because at that time, I was in prophetic training. Every prophet needs to know how it feels to be in a status quo church and get kicked out. That is part of the training.

I grew up in an apostle's home. Yet, God waited to send my family away so that I could join the status quo church and live everything that most other prophets live.

So, do not think that I have skipped one sliver of the death to the flesh that you have had to face. God made us walk through every single step.

During this time, I learned to become a wife and a mother. The Lord removed me from being too actively involved in ministry, where it would take up my time. Then, once I had learned to submit to my husband and love my children, God opened the way for us to come over to Mexico and join the work.

MARRIAGE AND FAMILY AND WOMEN APOSTLES

CHAPTER 02 – MARRIAGE AND FAMILY AND WOMEN APOSTLES

There are those that believe it is time for women to rise up and take their place in the church. Then, you have others who believe that it is absolute heresy for women to do as little as teaching in the church.

There are two dramatic extremes. As I came to prepare this message, I said, "Lord, how am I going to bring balance to these two extremes?"

The truth is that there is so much teaching on it, with really good arguments on both sides. This is not that kind of book. Rather, let me do what God has called me to do and help you along your own journey.

You must realize that God is revealing a mystery to His church, to His End-Times apostles today. It was just as He did for Apostle Paul.

In Apostle Paul's day, he knew that the Gentiles would be used of God. Who knew that the Gentiles would come into the Church? What a mystery!

They had no clue. It was not until Peter went in and led Cornelius and his family to the Lord.

Paul said, "The Lord has revealed to me a mystery."

That was his mandate.

Yet, there comes another mystery, and that is the End-Times Church.

> *God is raising up His apostles in this day and age to reveal this new mystery in the body of Christ. Part of that mystery is that God is using women in the End-Times Church.*

We are not in an era like we were in the New Testament. Yet even in the New Testament, thousands of years ago, we see God starting to use women.

Do you know how miraculous that is, just for their names to be mentioned in Scripture?

In a society where women had no vote or place, that was very uncommon.

Now, multiply the fact that we live in a society today where women not only have a vote, but also leadership positions in business, arts, and the world. It is no longer uncommon to see women in positions of influence.

It has released God's hand to raise up women, to use women. You see, God was never the problem.

God had no problem using Deborah in the Old Testament. He first just needed the king to want to work with her. When the king needed her, God said, "I will use the woman." (Judges 4). Now before we get too high-minded, think on this.

> ***Ephesians 5:24*** *Therefore, just as the church is subject to Christ, so let the wives be to their own husbands in everything.*

Do you think that because you are a woman apostle that you can take that scripture and throw it away?

WIFE — TRAINING IN MARRIAGE

If I am going to fulfill the mandate that God has on my life, I need to fulfill every single aspect of the Word of God and leave nothing out. God would not release me into ministry until I came to that point of submission.

I had to let go and say, "Lord, not my will, but Yours be done."

If my husband said, "No, we are not going to Mexico. We are not doing ministry."

Then, I would wait on God to move.

Fortunately, I married the right man. Thank the Lord. He was also in prophetic training at that time. When the call came, it was unanimous. We both knew that this was what God wanted.

God had already made us into a team and a family. God could begin to work in our lives.

I already had a foundation from growing up in the Lord, and from all the teaching that I received. I added a piece to that foundation by having a husband and by learning to submit and be a wife.

MOTHER — TRAINING IN FAMILY

> **Titus 2:4** *that they admonish the young women to love their husbands, to love their children, 5 to be discreet, chaste, homemakers, good, obedient to their own husbands, that the word of God may not be blasphemed.*

Then, I had some children and learned to be a mother. I had to learn to get my own home in order before stepping out and trying to get the body of Christ in order.

What kind of foundation was I going to launch off if my own home was not in order? That is not God's pattern at all. You can look from the Old straight through to the New Testament and see that there is no place for a loner.

Even Moses, as great as he was, had Miriam, Aaron, and Joshua.

David had all his mighty men.

Jesus had His twelve Disciples.

Was I just going to rise up and be this great woman apostle all on my own?

That is not God's pattern. He said to me, "First, you will learn to be a wife and a mother. Once you have learned that, I will teach you to mother my Church. I will teach you how to be an example in my Body.

Yet, first you must learn your place of submission in the home. As you learn that place of submission and respect for your husband in your home, I will raise your husband up to cover you and open the doors before you."

Let me tell you something. There is not a step that I take in ministry where my husband is not opening the doors for me and standing behind me.

With every affront that I have to take, he is there, one hundred percent behind me.

When I have men coming to me saying, "By whose authority do you stand up to speak?"

I just grab Craig and say, "Would you like to speak to my husband?"

We came to Mexico, and we were given the opportunity to receive, as a couple, from my parents.

It started off first as relationships of mentorship. Being that he was also my natural father perhaps made it easier in the sense that I could not run away.

I could not say, "That's it! I'm sick of all this death. I am out of here."

He was my natural dad. I had to hang around.

My father mentored us both, and the first phase that we went into was into prophetic office. Before we left South Africa (1998), he released us into prophetic training, and that was the only knowledge that we had of the prophetic or apostolic at that time.

All we knew was that there was a training phase. My father had experienced it for himself, so we were somewhat prepared when he released us, but not as prepared as we could have been.

When we landed in Mexico, we had already gone through our phases of training, and we were placed in office. Then, he taught us how to function in that office. Suddenly, God started revealing all this other stuff.

We learned about apostolic types and so much more. It was mind-blowing.

What was an apostle?

I kind of thought what everybody else thought. If you want to know about the apostles, you need to read the New Testament. The apostles are not for today.

However, God had a plan. As the Lord changed us and mentored us through my parents, He brought a whole new dimension.

SPIRITUAL DAUGHTER — MENTORSHIP AND PARENTING

He started showing us about spiritual parenting.

> *1 Corinthians 4:15 For though you might have ten thousand instructors in Christ, yet you do not have many fathers; for in Christ Jesus I have begotten you through the gospel.*

God started to show us that there was more than just mentorship, but also spiritual parenting. We came to a point of realizing that the relationship that we were in was not just a mentorship relationship, but a spiritual parenting one.

My father was laying a foundation in us, teaching us how to do the work of the ministry and then releasing us to do it. There came a last missing piece of my foundation.

You see, Paul said, "I suffer not a woman to preach in my churches."

My apostolic father stood up and said, "I suffer a woman to teach in my churches."

If someone came to me and said, "How can you stand up and teach?"

I said, "You can take this up with Craig and with my father."

I suggest Craig though, because he is nicer.

> *I do not stand here by my own authority. I stand here under the authority of my husband, and above all, in the authority of the Holy Spirit, the Lord Jesus Christ, and the Father.*

THE TEST

When I was first placed in apostolic office, the Lord gave me a test.

He said, "Colette, a time will come when you will go to a place where they do not receive women. They will not allow you to teach, to be called apostle, or even to be called a prophet.

However, you will go into those places, and you will minister as an apostle and will stand in the authority of an apostle. You will bring change as an apostle. Yet, the people will never know that you are an apostle, though you have completed an apostolic work.

Are you prepared to submit to these terms and conditions?"

I said, "Yes, Lord."

At the end of the day, what is it about? Is it about the titles that we wear, the recognition, or about the work that we are doing in the body of Christ? It is the work that we are doing that is going to cause the church of God to stand up as a city on a hill.

I hear so many women running around, moaning about not being received in their churches and not being accepted as women leaders.

Who cares whether they accept your title or not?

> *Rather take a lesser title, but stand in the authority, power, and anointing in the fullness that God has given you. Bring change to the body of Christ.*

Does it mean enough to you to put aside your recognition? Does it mean enough for you to put aside what you want and think?

In 2000, everyone wanted to be a prophet. It is still like that.

They think that it is a great honor, and they do not see that it is a call to death.

Now, everyone wants to be an apostle. If you say to someone, "I see that you have an apostolic calling," the next thing you know, they are calling themselves apostles.

Alright big mouth, if you want to call yourself apostle, are you prepared to pay the price?

If you are a woman, are you prepared to submit to your husband and to let go of your ministry for a season, so that you can submit one hundred percent to your husband?

This way, you can learn to be a wife and a mother. Are you prepared to really go through the training? Are you really prepared to pay the price?

Whether you like it or not, if you are to rise up as a woman in ministry, there is a greater price to pay.

> *The price is not to let go of your femininity. It is to stand in the fullness of your femininity, which includes full submission to authority.*

Until you can learn submission to authority, how do you expect others to submit to yours?

THE TRUTH ABOUT BEING AN APOSTOLIC WOMAN

It is time that there comes some balance in the body of Christ. We have this overswing of (can I say it...) dominating, single women.

This is my personal opinion, but I do not believe that a single woman should be standing up as a sole leader over any organization, without the support of a husband, an apostolic father, or a team.

Do you think that I am off?

Give me the name of any of the New Testament apostles that worked alone. Can you think of one?

If Apostle Paul, who wrote most of our New Testament, needed to work with a team, how much more a woman on her own?

If Jesus Himself, the Son of God, needed a team, do you think that you can stand alone?

There needs to be a balance in the body of Christ. God is raising up teams in His End-Times Church.

When you look at me, you want to know who stands behind me? My husband, my team, and the Lord stand behind me. When you come against me, you are coming against them first.

I stand united with an apostolic team, under the direction and the ordination of the Holy Spirit. You do not want to mess with that kind of support system!

Don't you think that it is time for us to see such teams rise up in the kingdom of God?

I do believe that there are many women that God is calling to leadership. There are women with fire. However, because you have not been prepared to go through these various phases of submission to your husband and get your house in order first, the enemy is destroying you.

If you have not learned submission, or to love with a mother's heart, how are you going to lead others to maturity?

You cannot stand there alone anymore. You think, "My husband will have to come right. I am going to get going in ministry and serving God."

Do you know what is going to happen?

THE STATE OF YOUR MARRIAGE

You are right. You have a fire and a call. Yet, when you go to stand up and be used of God, the minute that God uses you, satan will destroy your marriage.

There goes your whole ministry flat on the ground. How many more public ministers do we have to watch fall through their broken marriages?

I look at bold messages and think, "How can someone who claims to be used of God stand up and preach this, yet they are not living this at home?"

Take the time to allow the Holy Spirit to train you through your circumstances and challenge you.

Perhaps, if a man preached this message, he would get (a lot more) hate mail.

However, I am a woman, and I am a strong woman, capable and able. God has used me in so many areas, but this one thing I know: Without the skill of submission and servanthood, all of my ability means nothing.

That is where the power is. It is in your spirit of submission and love.

When you are fully submitted to your husband, and to your apostolic parents (if you have them), the hordes of Hell can try to come against you, but they will not get to you. You have protection.

NO MORE RENEGADES

However, there are so many renegades running all over the body of Christ right now. There are men and women alike. There are little wannabes here and there.

I am not denying the fact that you have a real call, but I question the foundation that you are laying, if you are not laying it clearly with a team.

If Jesus Himself used His disciples to lay down the New Testament for us and even needed to go through these phases, how much more do you need to learn to be a team and go through these phases?

This is one of the most outstanding differences that Craig and I believe very strongly in.

We do not believe that you should see just one apostle rising up with his name in lights. We believe that you should see apostolic teams rising up. In this way, each apostle will stand in the fullness of authority, working together and laying a foundation for the End-Times Church.

They will back and support one another.

You cannot walk the apostolic road alone. No one can, whether man or woman.

CHAPTER 03

APOSTOLIC MARRIAGE PREPAREDNESS

Chapter 03 – Apostolic Marriage Preparedness

Before the Lord can release you on the world and set you on your apostolic journey, there are a few things that need to come in line first. In fact, you have already been going through some of these things, but you have misunderstood them. You are in the throes of being positioned, but do not comprehend all the shaking and shifting.

Setting the Foundation Sure

The Lord is going to take you through a time of training in your marriage. You are going to be at the height of your call, and the Lord will suddenly say,

"Stop! No more ministry. Just stay at home and be a wife and a mother."

"Do nothing else, but invest into your family and love your wife."

"But Lord, shouldn't I be out there serving You and doing something magnificent?"

Alone, you are no use to God. The enemy can take you out so quickly. However, as a team, with your spouse by your side, everything will change.

That does not mean that your spouse will rise up to the same level of calling that you have. Yet, he should be able to not only support you, but minister to you, get revelation with you, pray with you, and open doors with you.

There are so many women that say, "My husband supports me. He has poker night on Fridays, and I have church on Sundays. He does not tell me that I cannot go."

That is not my version of support. That is not my idea of a relay team. The runners do not run off to the side and just say, "I will be there to support you by applauding while standing to the side of the track."

No, each one has a specific distance to run, and each one fulfills their function. That is teamwork. You need the kind of spouse that will support you, minister to you, and pour into you.

My heart goes out to you if you are caught in a bad marriage, but you cannot twist the Scriptures for a "work around".

Amos 3:3 Can two walk together, unless they are agreed?

Until your spouse stands with you in ministry to the point where he can pray with you, open doors with you, and minister to you and with you, then you need to forget about becoming an apostle.

Stay in the local church and minister in the capacity that you can. However, until your spouse comes to that level, God cannot use you in the universal Church. We are not talking about a body ministry here, where you can easily work under submission to a pastor. We are talking about apostolic office! One who is called to be a leader to leaders. Your covering needs to be sure.

Without this foundation, satan will destroy you and your marriage, and everything that you lay will be burnt up with fire.

The Lord cannot afford to entrust His people into your hands if you do not even have a tight team at home.

I know that this is a very harsh reality for some to face. I also know that it can be discouraging, but if you can learn to submit and love, God can change your spouse.

If He could change the heart of Pharaoh, He can change anyone. Your spouse does not have to be a great, big apostle like you. Yet, God does have a plan and a purpose for them.

That place is only going to be found when you sit down, shut up, and learn to submit and respect your husband.

God will move when a man truly loves his wife as his own flesh.

UNTIL UNITY IS ACHIEVED...

> ***Ephesians 4:1*** *I, therefore, the prisoner of the Lord, beseech you to walk worthy of the calling with which you were called,*
> *2 with all lowliness and gentleness, with longsuffering, bearing with one another in love,*
> *3 endeavoring to keep the unity of the Spirit in the bond of peace*

If you, as an apostle, are meant to be laying the foundation of the Church and bringing it into unity, how can you bring something to the family of God that you have not yet accomplished in your own life?

If you do not have the spirit of unity in your marriage, how will you build that unity into the Church?

> ***Ephesians 4:13*** *till we all come to the unity of the faith and of the knowledge of the Son of God, to a perfect man, to the measure of the stature of the fullness of Christ;*

When married, the two become one. According to Ephesians 4:13, we are to mature the saints to the point where we all come to a unity of the faith, where we are a perfect man.

You cannot accomplish this kind of wholeness without being one with your spouse. Are you beginning to understand why the Lord has brought you into the background for a season?

BEEN THERE... A FEW TIMES!

I already shared with you how the Lord drew me into the quiet before my training started, to learn to submit as a wife and learn to be a mother. Do not think that was the only time He did that. There came a time when I had tremendous success in my ministry. I was reaching many. As I began to publish my books, people were coming to us for ministry from all over the world.

I began to look more to the approval of my father than that of my husband. It was around this time that the Lord brought a dramatic shift to our ministry, and my parents stepped down and handed everything over to Craig and I (in 2009).

And so, now Craig and I had to learn to work together more than we ever had. I had leaned so much on my father, my husband had begun to take second place in my ministry and attention. Once again, God pulled us into the background.

Fortunately, we already had a ministry team in place to take care of the running of the work while He took Craig and I aside. For a full two years, we did nothing but work on our marriage. To fight things through. Heal things through. Rediscover who we were, and most of all... for me to learn to come, once again, under the covering of my husband.

If you think that you "get it once" and that is it, then you have some learning to do.

The more that God gives you, the more you need to learn to become a team.

God will always shift you around as a couple, and sometimes, He will switch your ministry roles completely.

Each shift comes with a new level of learning submission, respect, and love, to make sure that the enemy does not have a single foothold in your lives.

I cannot stress this enough. The Lord has prepared you for this calling your entire life. Will you really allow the enemy to destroy it at the core of who you are? I see so much failure right here. You invest so much into your ministry and others, that you forget without the solid foundation of your marriage, satan has all he needs to destroy everything God ever gave to you.

Are you beginning to see why God keeps pulling you aside and telling you to work on your marriage and family?

MARRIAGE TIME IS NOT WASTED TIME!

I work with a lot of leaders and prophetic trainees. When God sends them the message that they need to put everything on hold and invest into their marriage, nothing short of panic spreads across their face.

They feel that putting everything aside just for their marriage is a waste of time, time that they could spend ministering and time that they could spend "doing the stuff." Many become embittered at God and their spouse, not realizing that God just gave them the most precious gift ever!

God just gave you a training that will arm you in ways you cannot imagine. You will never go to battle uncovered. You will never stand in a storm alone. You will never again face the onslaught of the enemy singlehandedly.

With your spouse at your side, you will always have another person in this world to push through with you. However, if you do not invest into who you are as individuals, and also who you are as a couple, how can you arm up for war?

APOSTLES IN THE BEDROOM...

You have not even mastered the bedroom yet, and you want to take down the hordes of hell? Am I being too dramatic? Ok then, tell me how many prominent ministers have lost their ministry because they or their spouse had an affair? Still think that what goes on (or does not go on) in the bedroom is no big deal?

The more people you reach, the more your marriage will come under attack. So, take the time that the Lord is giving you, and treat it as the gift that it is!

Jesus turned the world upside down in just three years. I am pretty sure that even if you spent 10 years working on your marriage, the two of you would still have another three of which God could use to do something amazing.

If God has shut open doors and not allowed you to
step into leadership, or what you consider to
"move forward in your call", then sit down and
start listening. He has you in this place for a
reason.

Invest into your marriage. Take hold of the marriage tools that
you can. Work through your conflicts. Get on the same ministry
page. Work through until you come to "unanimous agreement."

A Word Based Example

There is no greater example of this kind of teamwork than that of
Aquila and Priscilla:

> ***Acts 18:26*** *So he began to speak boldly in the synagogue.*
> *When Aquila and Priscilla heard him, they took him aside*
> *and explained to him the way of God more accurately.*

Apollos was fired up and preaching all about the baptism of John.
So, along come Aquila and Priscilla to teach him correctly. In fact,
this couple is specifically mentioned together six times in the New
Testament. Apostle Paul called them both his fellow workers.

So, while Apostle Paul did not "suffer a woman to preach", he
allowed Priscilla to preach to Apollos alongside Aquila. Paul then
went on to work with them and sent greetings to the church in
their home.

Speaking as a Woman...

So, even Apostle Paul, who was adamant that a woman should
not instruct a man, could allow Priscilla to do so under the
covering of her husband. I love this balance, and now, speaking as
a woman (and not an apostle), I feel relieved. It means I do not
need to do this all alone.

When I stand in the anointing and power of God when He uses
me, realize that I do not live there 24 hours a day. Sooner or later,

I must come down from the mountain, and there are days that I am weary of climbing. There are days when the hordes of hell overwhelm me.

There are days when the rejection and opposition outweighs my faith, and I begin to waver. In these moments, I am just... a woman. I am weak.

The warrior is a child that needs strong arms to run to. In these moments, I thank the Lord for the years He set Craig and I to work on every conflict and struggle.

Because in these moments, I can just be... a woman. Not an apostle. Not all anointed and appointed. I can be the person I am, without the power. I can rest a while.

> *Jesus often said to His disciples, "Come aside to rest...". We all need that rest, and God has given us the gift of marriage to find it.*

So, when the voices of accusation are loud, my failures are staring me in the face, and I cannot pick my sword up any longer, I lie in the arms of my husband and let my tears fall. He does not always have the answers. He understands but cannot make the journey any easier for me.

Then again, He does not need to. I do not need him to be the Holy Spirit to me. I just need him to be my husband and complete me where I am weak, and to soften me where I am strong.

THE APOSTOLIC MOVEMENT – ARE YOU READY?

CHAPTER 04 – THE APOSTOLIC MOVEMENT – ARE YOU READY?

In Mexico, the houses are not built for rain. We discovered this in the first year that we moved there, when we had our first real thunderstorm. We sat without electricity for a couple of days.

We thought, "That happens sometimes. Next time, it will be better."

No, the Santa Ana winds started to blow, and power lines began to sway. There was a lot of flickering, and the lights went out again.

We discovered that this was just the way things were in Mexico.

We fought it for a while, blaming it on the devil and the weather. One day, we came to a conclusion that this was just the way it was. We just needed to buy a generator.

The next time that the winds blew, the rain fell, and the thunder began, we were the only house in the neighborhood still watching our movie.

There were some important things that we needed to get wired up. We needed a light, internet connection, and the television. What else can you do when all the electricity is out?

The point is that we learned to prepare. Sooner or later, the storm was going to come. We did not know when or how often it was going to come.

However, there was something about that generator in the backyard that made me feel secure. When the rain did come, I was fully prepared for what would happen.

THE RAIN – FORMER AND LATTER RAIN

> *Joel 2:23 Be glad then, you children of Zion, and rejoice in the Lord your God; for He has given you the former rain*

faithfully, and He will cause the rain to come down for you — the former rain, and the latter rain in the first month.

24 The threshing floors shall be full of wheat, and the vats shall overflow with new wine and oil.

Joel 2:28 *"And it shall come to pass afterward that I will pour out My Spirit on all flesh; your sons and your daughters shall prophesy, your old men shall dream dreams, your young men shall see visions.*

29 And also on My menservants and on My maidservants I will pour out My Spirit in those days."

Rain is coming to the Church! The former and latter rain is coming, not just the latter rain. Are you prepared for it? Now, we have already spoken about preparing your marriage and family for your apostolic call. This enables you to be positioned correctly to be used of God as He moves forward in the Church.

However, now that your boots are on the ground, it is to get yourself focused on the prize of the upward call in God through Christ Jesus (Philippians 3:14).

God is moving in His Church. He began moving some years ago. Through generations, there have been prophets who have spent hours on their knees, interceding for the move of God that we see in this day and age.

They have interceded through the Middle Ages and through the various revivals. Do you think you are the first to come? What we see now is a generation of prophets that have been birthed on the knees of God's people.

Today's prophetic move was birthed through generations of people praying in their secret place, who would but dream to see what we freely walk in today.

Others were persecuted for what they believed in.

Apostle Paul said to the Church, "You get to experience the mystery." (Rom 16:25).

In Hebrews 11, it says that, although the fathers of our faith had obtained a good report, we see and walk in the promise they never had!

We, in our generation, get to see what generations before us never saw. God has a plan for His Church. The rain is coming. Are you prepared?

No, I do not care if you believe in the fivefold ministry or not. I do not care if you believe in apostles or prophets. Are you ready for the rain? Because it is coming, whether you believe in it or not.

PREPARE FOR RAIN

If you want to stick your head in the sand - knock yourself out. The fact remains... the rain is coming.

If you think that not believing it will stop the clouds from forming, you are in deception. This move has been prophesied for generations. It is time that we see the fruition of what God has promised us for years.

He has been knocking on our doors and warning us. Even now, there is a rumble in the earth. You feel the rumble. The problem is that you do not know what to do with it. You are not prepared.

You want God to bring the rain in your bucket, in your way. When the rain falls, it falls where it wills. Are you prepared to catch it the way that God needs you to? Are you prepared to channel it to where it needs to go?

In this new move that is coming to the Church, there are many different aspects that God is setting into place. The body of Christ sometimes looks a bit like a dismembered body. All these bits and pieces do not make a lot of sense, but it is coming together.

To discuss every aspect of what God is bringing to His church would take a lot longer than just one chapter. So, I am going to speak about two specific aspects of what we are seeing being resurrected in the Church and your part to play as an apostle.

I am not talking about something new being birthed. This is not something new. This is a resurrection of a vision, the former and latter rain. There is only a latter if there is a former. We had the former. It is called the New Testament Church.

A MYSTERY IS BORN

Have you ever wondered why verse 28 above said, "It will come to pass afterward that I will pour out my spirit upon all men?"

At the birth of the New Testament Church, we saw an outpouring of the Spirit. We saw a mystery being born. It was something that could not have been anticipated. Yet, when the Apostles went back and looked at the Old Testament, they saw the truth that had been staring them in the face all along.

Are you prepared to look at the truth that has been staring you in the face all along? It is time that we complete the pattern that the Apostles began in the New Testament Church.

Even now, God is raising up His fivefold ministry. Although the term might seem new to you, the concept is really not anything new.

I see people writing and saying, "The fivefold ministry is the latest fad!"

Where have you been? It was there two thousand years ago. Time to catch up.

This is not the birth of a new vision. This is a resurrection of what has been with us. We, today's Church, stand at the threshold of participating in something that the apostles of old could only imagine.

RESURRECTION OF A VISION

I wonder, could Paul have envisioned what we see here today? Did he see it when he was sitting in prison, putting pen to paper, pouring out the wisdom that God had given him?

He reached one soldier after another for Christ. Do you think you need to reach the whole church of thousands of members from the pulpit? Paul had a pen and a parchment, and the odd prison guard that came to take care of him.

Paul was saving the whole of Caesar's household from prison. They had to keep switching out the guards. He mentioned quite a few of them.

Could you be caught saying, "Paul was not much of a leader those days. He only helped one man at a time. What could a man like that accomplish?"

I wonder, if he could have seen into the future and looked into our faces, if he could have imagined the extent of the Church today.

The Apostles paid a very high price with their blood for the pattern that God had for His people. Are we prepared to take the baton that they have passed us and carry it to the next generation?

> *It is time for the latter rain. Whether you are ready or not, the rain is coming. God waits for no man. Do not think that He is sitting on His throne, waiting for you to get a clue.*

If you do not want to step up, He will find someone else who will. Have no doubt, the rain is coming.

There are two main elements that I see God resurrecting in this End-Times Church.

1. Restoration of Spiritual Parenting
2. Restoration of Fivefold Ministry Teams

It sounds so progressive, right? Spiritual parenting and fivefold ministry teams!

If I said to Paul, "Check this out. We are so progressive."

He would say, "What? This is what I did."

Forget progressive. You need to go back and pick up what you have put down. If we want to see the power in today's Church that they saw in the Early Church, then we better take a few pages out of their book.

CHAPTER 05

RESTORATION OF SPIRITUAL PARENTING

CHAPTER 05 – RESTORATION OF SPIRITUAL PARENTING

How about we model ourselves after our models? How about we model ourselves after Jesus? He lived and ate with at least twelve men. There were even more because, on the Day of Pentecost, there were a lot more than twelve gathered in that house.

He shared His life, day in and day out, for three years. He parented, imparted, and discipled. God is restoring this vision and pattern to the Church in today's day and age.

Suddenly, all these shifts and nagging children that God keeps dropping at your door makes sense. You are tripping over them.

"What is going on? Another one? Where are all these babies coming from? Lord, what are you doing?"

You are trying to make your way to the pulpit, and you can hardly get there because of all the orphans that He is putting at your feet.

> *It is time to get the memo. God is restoring spiritual parenting to the Church. He is placing a call on your life that the likes of Peter and Paul walked in.*

Do you understand the weight and responsibility? This is not an annoyance or a sidetrack. This is the pattern for God's Church.

I have good news for you. The latter is going to be more glorious than the former.

What we saw in the New Testament Church is but a taste, a glimpse of the power that we will see in the Church. This anointing is not just for you and me, or for select leaders. This is for every single believer in the body of Christ.

We are to be a city on a hill, not a pillar on a hill. How are we going to establish that city unless every believer is walking in miracles, power, and the glory cloud of God?

That is going to take a bit of spiritual parenting.

OUR MODEL – APOSTLE PAUL

> ***Romans 16:21*** *Timothy, my fellow worker, and Lucius, Jason, and Sosipater, my countrymen, greet you.*

They were not always spiritual son and father. They started out as fellow laborers. There is such a different tone when we go to 1 Corinthians 4. We start out as Timothy, my buddy whom I serve the Lord with. Then, a shift comes...

> ***1 Corinthians 4:15*** *For though you might have ten thousand instructors in Christ, yet you do not have many fathers; for in Christ Jesus I have begotten you through the gospel.*
>
> *16 Therefore I urge you, imitate me.*
>
> *17 For this reason I have sent Timothy to you, who is my beloved and faithful son in the Lord, who will remind you of my ways in Christ, as I teach everywhere in every church.*

He says, "I want you to be imitators of me. However, just in case you do not know what I look like, I am going to send Timothy to you. I am sending him because he looks and preaches like me. You can receive from him and be receiving from me."

Can you say that of those that you have fathered, discipled, and raised up? How many can you send to another church and say, "I cannot make the meeting, but take my son, Timothy, he will show you what I am about?"

It is a price to invest that trust into somebody else. It breaks a couple of boundaries, doesn't it? How else are we going to change the Church?

We have someone with an incredible anointing on their life, a fantastic vision. How are you going to spread that vision throughout the body of Christ, unless there are five, six, or seven of you (at the very least)?

Paul got that. He knew that he could not always be there. He knew that he could not be in every church. There was a whole world to be reached.

He thought to himself one day, "I need more of me. If there was more of me, I could double my reach."

The world even gets this concept. That is the sad truth. The Church is still lagging behind because that means, "Someone else will get the glory that was meant for me."

How are we going to change the Church if we are stuck in Jerusalem? The Holy Spirit came on the Day of Pentecost. Jesus said to His disciples, "Go forth and reach the world. Go to Samaria and the uttermost parts of the world."

They were so excited, and then the scripture right after that said, "They gathered together in Jerusalem." (Acts 1:8).

"You guys have a great Jerusalem going on here. I love Jerusalem. Jerusalem is the bomb. Everything happens in Jerusalem."

"Do you want to know what's going on? You need to go to Jerusalem!"

It is great that Jerusalem got saved... just a pity about the rest of the world.

THE MIGHTY SCATTERING

So, God sent an angel from heaven who went by the name, Saul of Tarsus, to scatter the Church. They had to run for their lives. There is nothing like a little fire behind you to make you run.

Do you know what happened then? They started spreading the word. It was so amazing. They took all the doctrine of the Apostles - everything that the Apostles had imparted to them.

Wherever they ran, they dropped coals of fire. The next thing you know, a church in Antioch sprung up out of nowhere. It was not founded by any apostle or evangelist. These were just believers that were so on fire and had received the fullness of the impartation of the Apostles.

Tell me – if you let your church loose, would there be fire?

What if your church was scattered? Would they take coals with them and ignite this world? Have you imparted and entrusted that much to them that we, together, can change the world?

You are sitting in little Jerusalem with a nice little church and structure. You have a little warm fire to keep your hands warm.

> *God does not want a toasty fire. He wants a raging inferno!*

I want to see the body of Christ rise up in power. I want to see a city on a hill that is drawing in the nations. I want to have our banner waving so high that the world around us sees.

I want them to be drawn to us, like moths to a flame.

THE CHURCH AT ANTIOCH

The church in Antioch was born, and the Apostles had to send some people out. Isn't it amazing that the very man who caused the scattering, causing Antioch to be birthed, ended up making this his home town?

Antioch became Paul's headquarters. He came back to Antioch again and again. God has a sense of humor. Paul was being used of God, while unsaved as well as saved.

This process is only going to take place through spiritual parenting.

> *2 Timothy 2:1* *You therefore, my son, be strong in the grace that is in Christ Jesus.*

2 And the things that you have heard from me among many witnesses, commit these to faithful men who will be able to teach others also.

Therein is the pattern for the End-Times Church. Who have you entrusted with the gold that is within you, that they may in turn entrust it to others?

When you die one day, will your message die with you?

Does the word and vision that God has given you die with you? Have you passed it on so that the flame may continue to be nurtured, from heart to heart, continually growing?

The call of God is without repentance, but it does not mean that you are the only one that can carry that call out. You are dispensable, but the call will remain.

Will you pick up the call? If you will not, you can be sure that there are others who are hungrier than you. However, right now, you are in a position where God can use you, so He will come to you first.

Yet, if you do not pick up that baton, He will find someone who will, because He is God. This is His Church and pattern that He has promised us since the beginning that He would bring.

He promised that He would bring us the former and latter rain. No matter what happened to Paul, even after he was beheaded, the word he taught continued.

How do you think we got the Bible in the first place? Who do you think gathered those parchments and made sure that they were kept?

It was the elders who wept upon him on the beach. They clung to him when he said, "This is the last time you will see my face. Stop weeping. You are breaking my heart."

It was those who took those parchments with their life and guarded them. They passed them from church to church. Is that what your ministry is doing?

That is the pattern for apostolic office.

Yet, you are clinging to your little parchment.

"I have a great vision."

So does everyone else. What are you doing with your vision?

God has given you something incredible. It is not just for you. Unless it is handed out, how will it ever bear fruit? Unless the seed is planted into the soil and dies, it will not bring forth fruit.

You are afraid to see the seed die. You are afraid to plant the seed into hearts that will consume it and cause it to die.

So, whose seed is it again? Isn't it God who gives seed to the sower?

TIME TO SOW YOUR SEEDS

He gave you the seeds to sow. Do you have them in your cupboard, or have you put them into hearts?

When you put them into hearts, sure enough, there are some that birds will come and steal, and some that will land on a rocky heart. There are some that the weeds will rise and choke. There are also some that you will sow in fertile soil, and you will reap.

There will be a thousand-fold return, and that one will take those thousand seeds and sow them and experience the same thing.

Not every seed will flourish. Do not be in delusion. You and I both know the truth. Yet, just because one seed dies, does that mean that you stop sowing?

Can you imagine a farmer that sows three seeds? Then, he waits and says, "There is no wheat this season. I may as well give up. These are bad seeds."

You only sowed three seeds – what did you expect?

He does not only sow a couple of seeds and stop and wait to see what happens. He throws out as much seed as he can, because he knows what is going to happen.

He knows that the birds will get some and that some will never make it through the soil. He sows them all out. Out of all those seeds, the ones that take root are the ones that produce the crop.

I know that you have sown seeds in vain, on hard soil. You have even had some throw your seed back at you.

Does that mean that you should stop sowing? Does that mean that the pattern is wrong? Just because some did not receive it, does that stop the rain from falling?

YOU CANNOT DO IT ALONE

Paul knew that he could never do the work alone. You know that too, but are you willing to pay the price to do the work that God has given you?

You know that you cannot do it alone. You feel your own limitation, but you are trying to reach out within that limitation, instead of breaking loose and paying the price that God is asking you to pay.

You need to give without reserve. You need to allow yourself to be hurt and disappointed for the sake of one seed that will flourish. That will be your reward.

What you do in secret, your Father will reward you for openly. When your faith is in Him, you can be sure that He will water the right seed at the right time. Out of all those that you trip over and that God brings you, you may just have one Timothy.

Do you know that is all you need?

> *You just need one who is prepared to take what*
> *God has given you and pass it onto the next*
> *generation.*

That is why, even now, I am seeing God raise up family teams, husbands, wives, and children. Who better to pass that on to?

If Paul would have had a son that continued in the ministry with him, I can imagine that he would have been the Timothy.

Not all of us have that opportunity, but with the work that we are doing, we are seeing God raise up so many different couples. We are seeing the Lord raising up families to stand up and be counted.

Do you want to know how this work is going to continue? It is going to continue when we pass it on. When that passing on stops, the fire stops, and God has to start all over again.

RESTORATION OF FIVEFOLD MINISTRY TEAMS

CHAPTER 06 – RESTORATION OF FIVEFOLD MINISTRY TEAMS

Acts 15:40 But Paul chose Silas and departed, being commended by the brethren to the grace of God.

Paul knew that he could not do it alone. Even though he had a spiritual son, he actually had a lot more than that. Timothy was not the only one that he worked with. Though, I would daresay that Timothy was the one who got all of his spiritual DNA.

Timothy got Paul's anointing and doctrine. Everything that Paul was, Timothy became. I can imagine that if you saw them walking down the street together, they probably would have had the same limp.

They must have pulled the same kind of face. There is something about when you rub off on people. You start pulling the same faces and saying the same things. I can imagine that people thought Timothy was his natural son.

It is because of how much he received. Yet, Timothy was not the only one that Paul worked with. Paul also worked with Silas who was a prophet.

PAUL AND THE FIVEFOLD MINISTRY

Paul knew what it meant to work with the fivefold ministry. They all worked together as a team.

Philip went ahead spreading the word and bringing fire. The apostles came afterwards, laid hands, and brought the indwelling of the Holy Spirit. Then, Paul came along to teach, and Silas to motivate and encourage.

Each of them played a part. It was beautiful and seamless. They did not put much thought into it. In fact, when you read the book of Acts, Luke rambles on, assuming that they obviously know what is going on.

It was so uncomplicated. They flowed from the Spirit and walked in the Spirit. When they walked in the Spirit, they did not fulfill the lusts of the flesh. They just did what God inspired them to do.

Each of them had their own place. There was no competition of everyone trying to be a prophet, or everyone trying to be a teacher. They all did what was in them to do. As the Holy Spirit manifested each gift in them, they walked in that gift.

Yet, somewhere down the line, we found it too simplistic for us.

We decided to complicate it.

Bit by bit, the anointing began to wane in the Church, and a scattering took place.

God's man for the hour started to rise up. We went through the Middle Ages. The Church lost its footing, but it never lost its call. It never lost the pattern to be the city on a hill.

Now, we are feeling the rumbling in the earth, the foundation under our feet shaking. Even as you are reading this, you feel it. I am just giving you a glimpse of what it will look like.

We will once again worship in spirit and in truth, side by side.

Not by intellect and understanding!

We will naturally flow in the Spirit, without all of our junk. The pattern is already laid upon our hearts.

It is not like the Old Testament where you have to go by the letter of the law. You do not have to "cross every t and dot every i".

The law is on our hearts.

If you just stop and listen to what God has been telling you for years, you would be ten steps ahead already, but you are trying to intellectualize it. He never said that it is written on your intellect. It is written on your heart.

ENGRAVED ON OUR HEARTS

It is this annoying, churning struggle in your belly that you keep feeling and do not understand. You keep rebuking it, but it is God. It is His law trying to rise up out of you. It is His pattern.

He needs you to walk it out, and you will understand it later. The understanding will come. It is not like God wants to keep you stupid. He just wants to get you moving. He will give you the knowledge you need to walk it out, but you have to start moving first.

PROPHETS AND APOSTLES

The prophets and apostles are a special breed. Even now, the Lord is raising them up within the Church.

> ***Ephesians 3:4*** *By which, when you read, you may understand my knowledge in the mystery of Christ),*
>
> *5 which in other ages was not made known to the sons of men, as it has now been revealed by the Spirit to His holy apostles and prophets:*
>
> *6 that the Gentiles should be fellow heirs, of the same body, and partakers of His promise in Christ through the gospel.*

Paul is talking about something that nobody anticipated in the Old Testament. They knew that a Savior would come and that they would be set free.

When they looked at the Word, they could see that Jesus would die for the remission of sins and that He would redeem them. Yet, there was a mystery that Paul revealed.

In this passage above, Paul was saying, "There is a mystery that the Old Testament prophets did not know. There is something that we did not realize. The mystery that has been revealed is that the Gentiles will also come in."

Up until then, they thought that salvation was only for the Jews. That was until the experience with Peter, right? That was the mystery that the Lord revealed to him.

The Lord gave Peter a vision of a blanket coming down with unclean animals on it.

The Lord said, "Peter, rise and eat. Do not call unclean what I have called clean."

Then, Peter gets a knock on the door, and the first Gentile Christians come to Christ. They realize - salvation is for the Gentiles also. Check this contradiction out:

> **Acts 11:18** *When they heard these things they became silent; and they glorified God, saying, "Then **God has also granted to the Gentiles repentance** to life."*
>
> *19 Now those who were scattered after the persecution that arose over Stephen traveled as far as Phoenicia, Cyprus, and Antioch, **preaching the word to no one but the Jews only.***

So, after all the effort God went to, to reveal the mystery to them... they continued to preach to the Jews only. So, the Lord did what He loves to do. He sent a Jew of all Jews to go to the Gentiles.

That revelation came through the apostles and prophets working side by side.

God is trying to bring a revelation, and it is actually something that has been staring us in the face. He wants to bring a resurrection of His power.

That is why He is saying, "You need to start working together." It is because you need to bring the revelation to the Church. If you don't bring the revelation, who will?

BRING THE MESSAGE!

It is not for you to invite every other pastor and prophet to preach in your church.

You bring the message!

Why are you not bringing the revelation?

You should be getting this. God has it for you.

Apostle, if you would work together with the prophets, you could be raising up those that God has put at your feet.

Did Paul bring Peter in saying, "Please, come and preach at my church?"

They fellowshipped and were brothers, but Paul did not need that. He had enough revelation to go around. He worked together with the prophets. He had a foundation and a blueprint.

He did not need it. He was in touch with God. He knew what God wanted and where He was taking the Church. He was riding that wave. Are you riding the wave to go where God needs you to go?

It is only going to happen with a team. That is why you keep bringing other people in. You know that you cannot do this on your own. Yet, God is dropping at your feet the very people that can help you surf this wave.

He is trying to create a circumstance, here and now, to help you to achieve that goal. You are saying, "Why is the revelation not coming?"

It is because not all of the pieces are in place. That is why we are seeing a restoration of the fivefold.

What use is it for you to get the whole revelation, and you do not have people to slot into it yet?

You will get it a piece at a time.

Even the New Testament was not written in a day.

THE PROGRESSIVE REVELATION

That is how the mystery was revealed. It did not just pop up out of nowhere. They walked it out a step at a time until the penny began to drop.

They were continually moving forward.

That is what I feel the Holy Spirit urging you to do today.

You need to step forward into something new. Take a step out of your comfort zone, so that you can get a fresh revelation.

You do not need a prophet to come and give you a word from God. You can get it from God yourself, with the prophet, side by side. One can take a step and the other the next step.

You can confirm and back one another so that you can lay the foundation for the End-Times Church.

CREATING AN ENVIRONMENT FOR GROWTH

It is not going to be an overnight change. Jesus took three years. He was the Son of God. He was perfect!

I can imagine that He taught perfectly. He had all the anointing that He needed, and there was no limitation.

It still took Him three years, day in and day out with His disciples, in order for Him to raise them up. However, when He left, He laid the entire weight of the Church on the shoulders of just a few men.

That is quite a risk. You and I have paid our price. We have gone through the fire and done what we had to do, but can we really say that we have paid the price that Jesus did?

He went through a process to hand everything to twelve men that might make it.

He trusted the Holy Spirit in them to get the job done. He also trusted in what He put in them for the three years that they were with Him.

START WHERE THE PEOPLE ARE

It is going to take time and investment. Every church is at a different stage of progress. Where is your church and ministry at?

CREATING THE ENVIRONMENT FOR THE PROPHETS

CHAPTER 07 – CREATING THE ENVIRONMENT FOR THE PROPHETS

In some churches, there is an influx of prophets. In others, there are pastors, teachers, or evangelists.

It is not only the prophets that are rising up. All of the fivefold are rising up.

Where is your church at, and are you bringing the balance?

Depending on what the people need, God will bring enough to meet that need. Each of the fivefold ministry is going to bring the same message.

Have you noticed that?

OUR DIFFERENCE DEFINES US

> *You will get an evangelist, a teacher, and a prophet in a room. They will all say the same thing, but in a different way. They are meant to. It is the anointing that separates them, not the message.*

The message is the same. It is the way that they deliver that message that is different.

An evangelist will walk into a church and see the sin. He will see the unrighteousness. He will come with the fire of the Holy Spirit and speak about the spirit of the world, and demons will manifest. He will shake the church and call it to revival.

The teacher will do the same thing, but he will do it with the sword. He will say, "The Word of God says that the root of bitterness defiles many."

It is the same message delivered in a very different way.

Then the prophets will come and point out all the hurts and broken sheep.

Each one has the same message, but a different anointing. God is already starting to bring this to pass within the Church. It is for you, if you are an apostle, to create the environment for each one of them to find their place and fulfill their purpose.

CREATING AN ENVIRONMENT FOR THE PROPHET

The prophet is meant to bring the Church into a face-to-face relationship with Jesus. Let me give you a rundown of what prophets are meant to be doing. They are meant to be revealing Jesus to His people, not revealing themselves to the people.

They are meant to be helping believers find their place in the Body. You, as an apostle, have your structure and pattern that you have put in order. It is for the prophet to say, "I feel led of the Spirit that this person should be in this part of the structure. I see this vision, and this is where God has this person right now."

Then, it is for the apostle to say, "That is a good idea. Who can we use to train this person up in this capacity?

This person is very evangelistic, so let's find an evangelist to train this guy so that he can find his place in the Body."

The prophet may come along and say to the apostle, "I feel that the Lord is calling this person to be a teacher."

It is for the apostle to say, "Alright. What can we do about that? I have this division that I think this person will flourish in perfectly."

The problem, unfortunately, is that the prophet wants to do it all.

"I see that this person needs to be set in place. I am going to tell him that this is what he is called to. I am going to put him in place. I am going to lay hands on him, train him, and minister to him."

Then you wonder why you are butting heads with everyone. It is not for you to do all the work. We each play a part.

> *It is for the apostle to have the structure and pattern.*

When you each work together, it is so beautiful. Let me tell you, as an apostle, it is nice not to always get the revelation.

It is tiring. There are lots of people that we work with. Do you know how many people we work with at any given time? If I had to get revelation for every last one of them, I would be exhausted.

I do not have time to do that. I need to be on the mountain, in the presence of the Father, getting the pattern. I do not have time to be with Joshua down in the battlefield.

You, as an apostle, cannot do both. That is also where the confusion is. You see the prophets out there with the swords, doing battle, and you think that it is so cool. You would rather be in battle than on the mountain.

You would rather be out there trailblazing, on the cutting edge and looking cool with your sword gleaming in the sunlight.

However, you are just standing on the mountain, tiresomely shouting, "Go, Joshua!"

I was a trailblazer first. I liked being Joshua. He was so cool. We traveled, took the land, spread the word, placed people in office, and helped them find their place. Then, I ran off, not needing to care what happened with them afterwards.

That was my apostle's problem, not mine. Praise you, Lord!

I would just say, "This one belongs here. That one belongs there."

I just kept running. I loved being the trailblazer. It was like Paul said to Timothy, "You go out ahead of me and prepare the people. Then, I will come." I liked that part. I liked breaking new ground.

So, God would send me out to a new church or country. We would go and meet the people, start the work, and do all the exciting stuff. Then, the apostle would come and set the structure.

We would then go off to the next place, which was cool because I am expressive and love new people, sights, and food.

Off we went again. I thought that I could do this forever. This was my life.

Then, I became an apostle.

The Lord said to me, "Moses!"

"Yes, Lord."

"What are you doing down there in the trenches? Get yourself on that mountain."

"But, Lord, I like it down here. I love the sight of blood in the morning. I live for this stuff."

"It has changed. If you are always in the trenches, how are you ever going to receive my pattern that I have given to you?"

He brought me some spiritual sons and daughters and some prophets to train up. They got to have all the fun. They got to meet everyone for the first time, deliver the words, go ahead, prepare the way, and break the ground.

I just came with the pattern.

You think that it is easy for the apostle to have the pattern?

"It's not fair! I also want the pattern."

There is a price to pay to be the one to get the pattern. It is boring up there. You just have Aaron and Hur.

You get to see things that they do not get to see.

Moses received an incredible pattern, but it was Aaron who went into the Holy of Holies. It was the family of Aaron that got to be the high priests, not Moses.

There is a high price to pay to be an apostle. A lot of the time that means stepping back so that others can take the land.

When it is taken, then you can walk in and say, "Good job. Now, let's put everything into place and bring structure."

In my team, the prophets especially, come to me and say, "Mom, this one has a clear teaching call."

I say, "Good. Put them under this trainer, take them through this module, and then report back to me once they have reached this stage."

"Mom, this person clearly has a prophetic call, but they are not ready yet."

"Put them in the Fivefold Ministry School. Have them do this curriculum. Watch their progress. If you feel that they are making good progress, we can switch them over to the Prophetic School. Get back to me when they are ready."

I do not need to do everything. I just set the structure in place.

"Mom, we have this invitation. What should I tell them?"

"What does our calendar look like? What do you feel in your spirit right now?

"I saw a vision of a new road when in prayer today. I feel God telling us to accept the invitation."

That is what I do. I set the structure and pattern. Every now and again, I have been known to pen a few words to paper and preach a bit...

However, they are the trailblazers. They are the ones that go out and break the ground. That is what the prophets are meant to be doing.

IS THE WORLD READY FOR THE PROPHET IN YOUR TEAM?

Now, if you are not investing into them, what is going to happen when you let them loose? Could you let the prophet loose on the world right now? Is the world ready?

That is the point. How else do you think that you are going to grow? Is it with your charisma?

Your charisma just goes so far. You are only one person. You need somebody to break ground for you. You need somebody to take what God has put in you and imitate you.

Once the ground is broken, you can come in and say, "Fantastic job! Here is the structure."

Perhaps you were the ground breaker. That was your passion. You wanted to break ground and start works. It was so cool. Then, it just fell flat.

"What happened to the anointing? God left me."

No, God is elevating you!

> *There is a higher call coming. It is time to train others to break ground. How else are you going to grow?*

You are one person. Instead of breaking ground in one church, you can be breaking ground in five churches.

What pattern has God given you as an apostle? What is your structure? That is what you should be getting on the mountaintop, like Moses.

Moses did not just go up the mountain once. He went up again and again, at least seven times. That is how he got the pattern for the Israelites.

In the same way, God will call you again and again to the mountaintop. Yet, if you are sitting in the valley, fighting the enemy, how are you going to get the pattern on the mountaintop? (In *The Moses Mandate*, I will take you through his journey in detail.)

You are too afraid to let that control go.

I know why you are afraid. It is because the prophets are not ready.

You and I both know what is going to happen. You are going to let them loose, and they are not going to break ground in accordance to the pattern that God has given.

BECOMING ACCOUNTABLE

So, whose fault is that?

You are the apostle. They are not the apostle.

If Aaron went into the Holy of Holies and did the job wrong, whose fault would it have been?

It would have been Moses' fault.

What would have happened if Moses did not tell Aaron how to enter into the Holy of Holies?

Aaron would have died, like his son did. However, Moses made it very clear, right down to the rings on the curtains.

Are people saying that you are nit picky?

Good!

You are in a good place. You better be nit picky because God has a clear pattern for you, and He will make you nit picky.

Do they have that structure of where they are meant to be going and what they are meant to be doing?

If they are not walking in that structure, you have not taught it to them, or perhaps you do not have a clue.

You are just hoping that they will wing it and somehow stumble across the Spirit, and it will all work out.

Let it go. It does not just happen.

It did not just happen for Jesus. He had a clear pattern of what was going to happen. Step by step, He warned His disciples.

"Guys, this is how it is going to go. I am going to die, I am going to resurrect, this is how it is going to happen, this is the structure..."

That is why Paul could say to Timothy, "You know me, down to the letter of the law that I teach. You are an imitator of me. Take the letter of the law, and pass it down to others, same structure."

No matter where you go in the New Testament, you will see the churches in the structure of either Peter, Paul, or one of the other apostles. They had a clear structure for others to move around in.

We think that structure stifles, but it does not. It brings freedom.

I know that you think bringing a structure will hinder the prophets, but you do not realize how much the prophets are asking for it.

That is why they are crying out for spiritual fathers and mothers.

They have all this passion. Since they are so pushy and loud-mouthed, you think that they will spew at you for hindering them with a structure.

It is you trying to squash their fire that is making them spit and spew.

The structure should give liberty, within a boundary. Not just because it is convenient for you, but a revelation from God.

When was the last time that you went through the Word and sought God for a structure of how you should handle those in your church?

Then, did you go to the church and say, "Guys, I have had a face-to-face with the Lord? From now on, I feel that we should minister in this capacity. I want you to take all that fire in you, and let's work together within this realm."

Your prophets will say, "Thank you Lord… FINALLY!"

They are like wild stallions. They are wild and crazy. Yes, this is true. However, that does not mean that they do not want to be part of this team of horses. They want very much to be part of this team.

It is in the heart of every prophet to want to be useful. It is because they hurt with the hurting and have so much hunger for the brokenhearted that they have so much passion.

Give them a structured opportunity, and you have just found yourself a Timothy who will stick by your side. You would have given them something that nobody else had the courage to give them – a place.

SETTING THE PROPHETS IN PLACE

I do not mean a place to prophesy, give prophetic words, and get revelation for people. I mean a place to help implement the structure that God has given you.

How many do you send out to preach, minister, and counsel?

You should have them do this, within the doctrine that God has given you. You need to give them the liberty to walk out their anointing, within your structure.

It is the price of the prophet to submit to that and to realize that this is their safety net.

You can be as prophet as you like within that structure. You can lay out all of that power.

They are crying out for this. Yet, they are misunderstood and over-emotive and causing a ruckus. A lot of them are even demonized.

DEALING WITH DEMONS

I remember a particular seminar that we had in Switzerland. We had to work through a translator. There was a lovely, young girl who the pastors had arranged to translate for us.

They introduced me to her and let me know that she would be translating for me.

I thought, "Oh no! There is a whole lot going on here. She has a heart for God, but there are some demons I am going to need to work through."

There was an hour to go before the meeting started.

They were going to stick me with this person. I was feeling those demons, and I thought, "I know myself. I am not going to be able to stand next to her without trying to deal with those demons."

I was not going to be able to preach.

I sat her down and said, "Ok, I do not mean any disrespect, but we have an hour, and you have demons. Usually, if I had the time, I would take you through the process, and we would work through it.

However, we really only have an hour. So, can we just deal with the demons because we need to stand up there, and I do not have time for this."

She said, "Praise God. That's the thing that has been holding me back!"

She was such a prophet, through and through.

She was hungry for God. Yet, nobody got in her face. They just avoided her. They said, "She has potential, but she also has these weird, quirky things, like... an angel of light."

Either they ignored her or squished her down. Nobody actually got into her face and said, "Let's deal with the demon."

So I come along with,

"If you want to interpret for me, then this is what I expect:

You will deal with the demon and flow in the spirit.

You will not make me wait.

You will speak right after I speak.

This is how we are going to work together."

She appreciated the structure.

She said, "Ok, I can do that. If that is what you expect from me, that is good."

Do your prophets know what you expect from them, or are you just waiting for them to "pick it up in the spirit" because they are prophets?

(I use the term "your prophets" very loosely. I do not imply that they are your prophets, because they belong to God. Rather, I am referring to the prophets in your team. It's just a whole lot easier to keep saying "your prophets" than "the prophets that are in your team." So, give me grace for the sake of brevity!)

They are not psychics. They are prophets.

One of my team members came to the breakfast table one time with a cloud over his head. He was grumpy, and it was not just because he did not have a good sleep.

I waited...

He pretended that everything was ok.

I said, "I am not a psychic. I am a prophet. Don't make me get revelation. What's up with you?"

Do your prophets know what you expect from them?

They really need that. They need to know if you do not like it when they do something.

They can deal with that. They just cannot deal with being ignored. It makes them feel unloved. It hurts them. Then, you take their hurt as rebellion.

Do they know what does and does not fly in your church?

You should be saying, "I recognize your call, and I appreciate what the Lord has put in you. However, you have a way to go. You need to grow up a little.

So, you need to go through a season of training. Then, we can get together again in a few months and talk again. Although I recognize you and appreciate what the Lord has put in you, you are not ready.

This does not mean that I will never give you an opportunity. I am just saying that if you are going to be used in the capacity that God has given me, there is a certain level of maturity that I expect from you."

You just set the playing field. They can decide if they like it or not, but you just set the structure. This way, you also weed out, right from the beginning.

You will not invest your heart into so many people who will end up saying, "That is not what I came here for," when you get to the crunch.

When you see someone that has a prophetic call, you can let them know how it is.

"I do not mind that you give a prophetic word. However, if you want to rise up into leadership, there are a few things that I am going to expect from you."

PROPHETS AND APOSTLES WORKING TOGETHER

CHAPTER 08 – PROPHETS AND APOSTLES WORKING TOGETHER

Every apostle will have their own standards according to the pattern that God gives them, however, let me show you what I expect:

> *1 Timothy 3:1 This is a faithful saying: If a man desires the position of a bishop, he desires a good work.*
>
> *2 A bishop then must be blameless, the husband of one wife, temperate, sober-minded, of good behavior, hospitable, able to teach;*
>
> *3 not given to wine, not violent, not greedy for money, but gentle, not quarrelsome, not covetous;*
>
> *4 one who rules his own house well, having his children in submission with all reverence*
>
> *5 (for if a man does not know how to rule his own house, how will he take care of the church of God?);*
>
> *6 not a novice, lest being puffed up with pride he fall into the same condemnation as the devil.*

Now, tell me something. If these are the qualifications for an overseer, how much more for a prophet?

Why are we not putting this expectation on the prophets?

Why are we allowing people to stand up, in ministry leadership positions, who do not have their home in order?

Does it fly for you, pastors? Apostles?

Did you receive the call of God and then suddenly see the doors just open, and you became a pastor overnight?

No. I sure know that this did not happen for me. I had to qualify. I had to go through fire. I had to learn the Word and study. I had to be qualified before I was given any position by God or man.

How about you? Did you just walk in one day and have handed to you a whole church on a silver platter?

I sure didn't, and anyone else in full-time ministry didn't either. They paid a price before God or man recognized them. So, why are we not laying this structure down for the prophets?

Should they not be more accountable than a deacon? Should they not be held to a higher expectation?

They give a prophetic word, so then that means that they get a pass because you feel the anointing?

DEFINING THE MINISTRY AND LEADERSHIP DIFFERENCE

The anointing is not good enough! Saul was also anointed. So much so that he was slain in the spirit, prophesying. Look where that got him. He was not obedient.

We misunderstand the difference between ministry and leadership. They have received the anointing, but do they qualify for leadership?

If you are in full-time ministry, you know the weight and expectation that people have when they stare into your eyes.

They look into your marriage, family, life, and how you handle money. They look into every last detail.

Yet, prophets can just stand up and prophesy because the anointing of God is on them? So, they can just stand up in the church, prophesy, and then go back to a broken home?

Would you be allowed to remain as a pastor or apostle if your house was in the same condition as the home of some of these prophets?

Apostle, what is your expectation? What is the pattern that God has given you?

By setting an expectation, you can see what you have to aim for. You can see the bar. You are not just going to be a prophet, but a leader in the kingdom of God.

You do not need to worry about the anointing. The Holy Spirit has your back there.

Moses did not need to wield the sword for Joshua. Joshua had that down. Moses just needed to give the pattern of how the structure was set in place.

You need to decide, with the Holy Spirit, what you believe is acceptable, not just for a prophet, but for a leader in your church. I am making this a little broader because the prophets are not the only ones needing guidelines.

All of the fivefold ministry is coming to you. Like I said, "The rain is coming."

Do you have that structure in place?

WHAT IS YOUR LEADERSHIP PATTERN?

What expectation and pattern do you have for someone to rise up in leadership in your ministry? Also, what are you going to do with them once they get there?

Are they just going to sit in the front chairs in the pulpit? What are you going to do with these guys?

Sure, they make you look good. However, you need a lot more than to just have people sit up front and give a prophetic word every now and then.

Were they not meant to be sent out, break ground, and mature the saints?

How about you come to the meeting and say, "This church is lacking in faith. I need a teacher to bring some teaching anointing to these people."

"You, come on! I need some anointing."

The church is down and discouraged, and they need a motivator.

"You, prophet... come. Motivate!"

This is why it is important that you have already set the structure for leadership, and what you expect from them, before they can rise up into that position. Now you know that you can trust them to stand up and represent Christ in your ministry.

From experience, I know that you do not grow any less.

They paid a price to get where they are. That is what a lot of prophets do not understand. This is what we try to teach them.

You think that a church leader just rose up overnight?

Do you think he said, "Cool, I cannot wait for the suffering and rejection, and to hear people tell me what to do? I cannot wait for the financial load.

I cannot wait for people to tell me that I am wearing the wrong shoes, not dressing right, and using the wrong words in my message. I cannot wait for people to tell me that I have offended them with a joke that I made."

We have all paid a price!

God made us pay a price, and our leadership made us pay a price. We had to study and show ourselves approved. We did not just waltz into it one day.

It is about time that the prophets also pay the price.

It is because we paid the price that we appreciate standing up there.

A Word to the Prophets

This is also why leaders fear giving the prophets that place.

"The pastor never lets anyone behind his pulpit."

Did you earn it, like they earned it?

When you have earned it with your blood, sweat, and tears, you will understand. It is a baby. As a mom, I am not going to hand my baby over to just anyone.

As a prophet, are you prepared to qualify and work with that leader and bear their child lovingly in your arms? Or, are you just going to hold the baby by the feet, complaining about how much you do not like it?

Do you know the price they have paid to bring that child into the world?

Now, you are just tossing it around and saying, "Do you know what an ugly nose your baby has? This is a deformed baby."

Maybe it is, but they have paid a price for that ugly baby. They are not just giving you their pulpit. They are giving you their heart.

What are you doing with it when you have it?

Are you crushing it and telling them that it is not good enough, pretty enough, organized enough, or holy enough for you? Are you telling them that it is not spiritual enough or Word-based enough for you?

They have travailed with the call on their life. They have failed and then got back up again. There were many around them that did not get back up again. Yes, they are not perfect, but they did not get here by mistake.

Then, you come as a little upstart with all your great ideas. Now, there is nothing wrong with your ideas or passion. We love your fire and anointing. We love to revel in the music when you pour out, and the spirit flows.

However, will you love that baby, even if it is an ugly one? Will you nurture the good in it?

WHAT YOU HAVE OVERLOOKED...

Perhaps the church is very status quo and stuck in its ways. It is ugly to you, but it is beautiful to the Lord and to the leader that nurtured it.

Yes, that baby needs to grow. Maybe you are the midwife, or the babysitter. Maybe you are the one to make it grow. Regardless, you better love it as much as they do. When you love it as much as they do, you are not going to need to fight your way to the pulpit.

They will feel safe to entrust their heart to you. They will feel safe to raise you up. They are not going to feel that they are going to raise you, and then you will say, "Now, let me show you something!"

The anointing is one thing. Spiritual maturity is another.

A WORD TO THE APOSTLES

You, apostles, swing from one to the other extreme.

There are those that have said, "I am not having any of that. You will sit down and shut up until I let you speak."

Then, you have others who are recognizing this move and anointing. Since you are sensing it so strongly, you feel compelled to just "let them at it".

That has backfired, because what comes out sometimes has not been the Holy Spirit.

There has been a spirit alright... just not the Holy one.

Instead of bringing healing to the church, it ended up bringing confusion.

As the leader, you are going to be like that shepherd who sees that wolf in sheep's clothing as a threat. That is your baby it is messing with.

However, if you set a structure from the beginning and say, "I see your passion, but if you really want to be used of God in this ministry and want to come alongside me, these are what the steps look like.

I do not care if they sound status quo to you. I do not care if you do not like them. Feel free to find another ministry that is even prepared to give you those steps in the first place."

When you set that structure, and they start climbing those steps, a relationship is going to form.

As a leader, when you see someone that has a hungry heart who is prepared to put that investment in, you keep your eyes open to see if they are a Timothy.

I wonder what will happen if I do not recognize them. I wonder what will happen if I say that I do not like that prophetic word. I wonder if they will still stick around.

You say, "That is unacceptable. That word was a deception."

They stick around and say, "Ouch! Ok, I am sticking to your heels."

"Hmm... you are going to pay the price, eh?"

If God has put you where you are, are you prepared to jump through the hoops?

"Why should I abide to the rules of man?"

God said so!

> **Romans 13:2** *Therefore whoever resists the authority resists the ordinance of God, and those who resist will bring judgment on themselves.*

PROPHETS...

I know that you see with different eyes, but you need wisdom, maturity, and leadership ability. The leader has that stuff. You may have the anointing, but you need the leadership thing that he has.

To get to that, you are going to need to climb the steps. It is not going to be comfortable. There is going to be some letting go of yourself.

At times, God may shift you. He may send you to another leader or apostle. Yet, are you prepared to be what God has called you to be?

The anointing is the easy part. The Holy Spirit has an abundance. He is not lacking in anointing. There are hundreds of anointings.

Yet, how many people in the Church today have the ability to walk it out with wisdom?

How many people have the ability to communicate that anointing in a way that people will receive it?

That is what your apostle should be teaching you.

APOSTLES...

You do not need to impart the anointing to the prophets or give them more revelation. You just need to tell them what they need to do to function efficiently in the pattern that God has given you.

It brings a rest. If you stop and think about it for a minute, you see what God has been trying to tell you.

You think, "That is why that was on my heart. I thought that was too restrictive. That is why I felt that certain way and thought that we should start doing this, but I did not get it."

If you can open a dialogue with your team, then you can share what is in your spirit with them.

"You are more than welcome to share with me what God tells you, but know this, I will wait on confirmation from God on that word to make sure that the timing is right.

Do not think that just because you have a revelation that I am going to jump. We are going to work this through together. I am prepared to listen, but are you prepared to wait?

Your word may not necessarily be wrong, but your timing may be. God is not finished with that word. There is more to it. Are you prepared to trust me as much as I allow you liberty?"

You can begin to work together now. They know where you stand, and you know where they stand. You know your boundaries, and they know their boundaries. They know where they have liberty, and where they are overstepping.

If they want to come into the next circle, you can tell them what they can expect for that also.

THE CHURCH WAITS... FOR YOU!

The Church is waiting for the apostles to set the structure.

The prophets are waiting for the liberty to express the anointing through that structure.

> *God is a God of order. How do you think that order is going to come to the Church, unless you bring it?*

The rain is coming. Moses, it is time to go up the mountain and get the pattern. It is time to go into the presence of the Father and allow Him to inscribe on your heart. You need to get the vision, the step-by-step instruction that He has for you.

Then, you can impart that to others. Do not expect them to give you the pattern. They are waiting on you. They do not have a revelation of the pattern. Their revelation will flow within the pattern that you receive.

How can God give them the right revelation if they do not have the right place to express it?

I feel the drawing of the Father. He is saying, "Come."

The mountain is shaking, and you are going in fear and trembling before Him.

He says to you, "Before you climb the mountain, you cleanse yourself, and let go of your baggage. Put down everything and come alone, Moses. Come into My presence and speak to Me face-to-face."

Stand in the midst of the cloud, with all of the noise around you, until you cannot see, hear, or understand anything except for the power of His presence.

Then say, "Speak, Lord. Your servant is listening."

Go there again and again as He draws you, and write the pattern down. A time will come for you to come down that mountain. Then, it will be time for you to implement it. By then, your Aarons will be waiting.

Hopefully, without a golden calf... but that is for another message!

Those prophets are waiting for you.

They are messing up in the mean time, going through their training. While they are going through their training, you can head up that mountain.

Perhaps you have been feeling this drawing away from the people and what you have done. Maybe you sense a deep rumbling in your spirit and find yourself distracted, like you should be engaged with what you are doing, but you feel a drawing.

You feel like the Father is saying, "Come away with Me."

He is calling you to the mountain. In the noise, it will be so quiet as His voice begins to speak to you.

THE VISION

The Lord gave me a vision many years ago. As I was in prayer, He showed me the world as a golden chess board. There were pieces that were cut out.

One by one, I saw the Lord put a piece in place, in each space.

When He put the last piece in place, a fire came in such power that it engulfed the earth.

He said to me, "Even now, in obscurity, I am training and raising up My mighty warriors. My apostles will find their place and add their piece to My pattern. When each one finds their place and establishes their pattern, I am going to send My fire on this earth.

There will be a revival and a move of My Spirit that the world has never seen before. This revival will not take place in one nation, city, country, or continent. It will be a universal revival that will erupt spontaneously in the same might and spirit as did my Early Church. This earth will know my name."

So, if you feel like you are dangling in the air, then you are right where you need to be, to be put in place.

Establish the piece that God has given you. Let everyone else worry about their piece. You just work on yours. Together, we are going to connect.

Wave your banner high, set your structure true, and let God move.

THE APOSTOLIC
MANDATE

CHAPTER 09 – THE APOSTOLIC MANDATE

As an apostle, God has called you to do something impossible. Do you think that it was in Peter's own natural strength that on the Day of Pentecost three thousand got saved?

In this day of knowledge, entrepreneurship, and all the resources that we have at our fingertips, I bet that each one of us could sit down and make a nice, analytical plan of what the Church should look like.

However, if this was something that we could do in our own strength, surely it would have been done already.

> *The reality is that standing in apostolic office is being called to do something that is impossible.*

This office is not able to be fulfilled with human hands, or to be built with your intellect, connections, or understanding. When you finally come to terms with that concept, you begin to realize that the call to apostolic office, and the call to fulfill the mandate that God has called you to do, does not rely on what you can do, what you have seen, or what you have accomplished.

It relies on the power of the Holy Spirit and the foreknowledge of the Father, who, since the beginning of time, has laid a foundation for the Church that will remain from generation to generation.

When Adam and Eve sinned in the Garden of Eden, the Father prophesied that...

> *"And I will put enmity*
> *Between you and the woman,*
> *And between your seed and her Seed;*
> *He shall bruise your head,*
> *And you shall bruise His heel." - **Genesis 3:15***

Generations ago, Jesus Christ and the walk that we walk today was promised by the Father.

This is not something that just happened overnight. This is a plan, a foundation that has been prepared since the beginning of time. It stands to reason then that this pattern requires a specific anointing and specific plan to fulfill.

This planning is not going to be made by man. Who, in all of their human logic, could have figured that through the death of one, many might be saved? The wisdom of this world is foolishness to God.

God is about to do something new in His Church. If you have an apostolic calling, listen to this carefully because this is your call to rise up. It is your call to responsibility. It is you that God is calling to rise up and take your place.

I ask you right now, are you ready to answer that call? It is time for the church of God to rise up. The time is now for this foundation to be built.

I think there is no greater allegory to use than that of the Temple. We are called the temple of God. Solomon built a grand temple based on the pattern of Moses and David – each a picture of God's pattern for His Church.

The pattern for the temple has been blueprinted a long time ago, and we have seen variations of it throughout the centuries. Apostle of God, our turn is next. When will we begin to build on its foundation?

THE TEMPLE MUST BE BUILT

I wondered to myself if, in the days of exile and captivity when the children of Israel and Judah had lost everything and been dragged away to Babylon that after seventy years of waiting, travailing, and being stripped bare, it even occurred to them that one day they would stand in a temple where the latter rain would be greater than the former rain?

You see, the Early Church was born in glory. Peter stood up on the Day of Pentecost, and the fire fell, three thousand were saved, and the Church exploded. People were added to the Church daily.

Next thing you know, Paul had a Damascus road experience, and churches started popping up everywhere. Antioch and Jerusalem were born as the disciples were going out. There was a massive explosion, and the pattern God established at the beginning was born.

Where is that Church today?

Satan was not too happy about that. So, he started to get the Church to compromise. If you do a bit of history, you will see that the Church was plunged into the Middle Ages. Yes, the Church was struggling along, barely alive, but who knew God's fire? It was so dead and scattered.

Just like God had taken the children of Israel and scattered them through the nations in the Old Testament, it seemed that believers were scattered in the same way. True believers with a true fire for God were scattered. What did the Church look like back in the Middle Ages?

The Church was warring with itself. You had the Catholics and Protestants at war with one another. Each new move was persecuted by the one that preceded it. With every new revival and message, there was someone else to come in and try to destroy it from within the Church.

The temple - the glory - was torn down. Everything was taken. The gold and silver was stripped bare until not even the foundation remained. Every wall that was built was torn down. All that remained was the rubble.

It seemed that the church of God was scattered to the four winds. You found little splinter groups scattered all over the place. We read their stories and see little revival healings here, little things happening in Indonesia there, and something happening in China there.

There are all these little scattered stories, but who is going to bring the Church together and build a new temple? When we do it, what will it look like? I daresay that our example comes from the prophecy of Ezekiel.

Now, before some are confused and think that I am talking about the building of a physical temple, let me reiterate. We are the temple of the Holy Spirit. I speak of a spiritual temple which is the pattern for God's End-Times Church.

EZEKIEL'S PATTERN

> *Ezekiel 43:10* *"Son of man, describe the temple to the house of Israel, that they may be ashamed of their iniquities; and let them measure the pattern.*
>
> *11 And if they are ashamed of all that they have done, make known to them the design of the temple and its arrangement, its exits and its entrances, its entire design and all its ordinances, all its forms and all its laws. Write it down in their sight, so that they may keep its whole design and all its ordinances, and perform them.*
>
> *12 This is the law of the temple: The whole area surrounding the mountaintop is most holy. Behold, this is the law of the temple.*

Now, Ezekiel lays out a pattern for a temple that has yet to be built. He goes through the length, breadth, height, cubits, gold, silver, and who is going to do what and how they are going to do it.

It has so many great details. However, the part that inspires me is in the part where the temple is complete. He says,

> *Ezekiel 47:1* *Then he brought me back to the door of the temple; and there was water, flowing from under the threshold of the temple toward the east, for the front of the temple faced east; the water was flowing from under the right side of the temple, south of the altar.*

*2 He brought me out by way of the north gate, and led me
around on the outside to the outer gateway that faces east;
and there was water, running out on the right side.*

The river did not flow through the temple, from one side to the
other, coming from some nowhere land. The river did not flow
into the temple. The river flowed from the very threshold of the
temple.

Then something happened as that river started to flow. It did not
start with a mighty rushing wind. It did not start as a waterfall,
hurricane, or tsunami. It started as a trickle that became ankle
deep, knee deep, and then waist deep, until you could swim in it
(Ezekiel 47:3-6).

As if that was not amazing enough that the temple originated the
water, what that water did was even more incredible. This is a
picture of the pattern of the Church that God wants to establish in
this time and age.

Why? Why should we build a temple that releases water across
the land?

Is it so that we can have a place to worship?

No.

Is it so that we can have more congregation members?

No.

So that our name can be written in lights?

No.

It is so the river can flow.

---

*There is a dying world out there, and they need
the river. Until the temple is built, the river cannot
flow. Until the apostles establish the pattern, the
apostolic anointing cannot flow and heal the land.*

So, dream with me a little about what this glorious Church will look like when it is finished.

Unless we have a vision of where we are headed, how do we know when we have gotten there?

REVIVAL IN THE DESERT

There are a number of things, if you read through Ezekiel 47, of what happened to the land as the river started working its way through. The first thing it says is that it went through the desert.

It went through the dry places first. This is such a beautiful picture of the revival that is coming to the world. You see, it did not say that the river went out and grabbed chunks of sand and dragged them to the temple.

"Let's get that sinner to church, brother. If we can get that sinner to church, the pastor can get them saved and Spirit-filled."

No, the water needs to go to the desert. Do not keep trying to bring the desert to the temple. The water needs to come from the temple and go out there. We are so busy having our little happy club that we have forgotten our purpose for building the temple.

The purpose for building the temple was not so that we could have a glory hallelujah. It was so that the river could flow outwards. You as an apostle are called to establish that.

"Lord, where is your glory? Lord, we need revival. Lord, we need your fire."

Have you built the temple?

"No, we are a bit too busy for that."

You keep on asking the Lord for more, but you are not getting a drop, never mind "more", until the temple is built. There is a whole world out there that sees you having your little happy club and does not know what that water tastes like.

It is so great that believers are running and splashing around in this water and having a fine time, while all along, there is a desert out there that does not know what the water tastes like.

When the Church has been established, we will see people being reached for Christ in places that we cannot imagine. Start thinking of the driest and most dead-boned places. Think of places where false religion is rampant. Think of the most impossible situation where there is no water or spiritual anything, and that is the first place that God is going to start His revival.

This is because if a revival started in the middle of a church, what glory would that be? However, if a revival started in the middle of a dry land - that would be impossible. That sounds like my God.

That is the kind of thing that He would do to make a point and to display His glory to the world. You keep looking for revival in churches, but you are looking in the wrong place. God wants to take His revival out there, to the world.

What needs to be brought to life but that which is dead? We are so busy trying to get a revival for our own feeling, and our own ministry, but it is not coming. You are getting frustrated. It is because you are asking for revival for all the wrong reasons.

The revival is not for you. It is for the desert that is out there.

TO HEAL THE SEA

The next thing that the river did was bring healing to the sea. You see, the sea has some water, but it is a pity about all that salt. You cannot drink it. This speaks of compromise in the Church. We have a whole Church of compromise.

They have been fed on the latest news, marketing programs, and doctrines from every internet, television, and media resource.

So, we have this really good water that we have contaminated with the spirit of the world. We have compromised our stand as

Christians. I am not just talking about one country either. I am talking about the Church universal.

If satan cannot dissuade you from serving the Lord, he is going to add some salt to your water. He is just going to cause the purity that you do have to become downgraded.

The next place where God will bring revival will be in His church. First, it will start out there, and then it will start in His church. It will come to those that have lost the purity of the vision that He gave them in the first place.

The End-Times Church is going to be a Church where being a Christian means something. When you say, "I am a Christian," they will say, "Wow! You are a Christian."

Back in the day when someone said, "I am an Israelite," that gave people a clear picture. They knew that with that came commitment, sacrifices, offerings, laws and commandments.

However, what does the word Christian mean to people today? It does not mean very much. It certainly does not mean born-again.

Yet, a Church is being born where it will mean something when you say, "I am a Christian." Christians will be set apart. They will stand as a city set upon a hill. Christians will be a lighthouse that those who are in darkness will seek our favor and come begging for the light that we have.

However, all that we are giving them right now is saltwater. Nobody can survive on saltwater. Some say to themselves, "My desert is better than your saltwater because at least I am having fun with mine.

You cannot decide what you believe. You have one foot in the world and one in the Church. Which one is it?"

I envision a Church where convictions are in the heart of every believer. They know what they believe, they know what Christ has given them, and they sense the spirit of God for themselves. They can discern what is right and wrong, and they are not dissuaded by every wind and doctrine.

They know what the Word says for themselves, and they are not running after pastors, prophets, and evangelists, trying to get a "have a good experience". They are bringing that glory themselves, and it is not restricted to one or two.

I see every believer walking in the fullness of the living waters that are inside of us. That is a picture of the future Church. Ezekiel says that the river brought life where there was death, a picture of those that have given up on serving God altogether.

They are not compromising. They are just backslidden completely. They have given up. They are dead. They have walked away. However, there will come life again. When you see a church, you will see a place of life and joy.

Switch on the news or walk to any newsstand, and there is death, destruction, fear, and this anticipation of doom across the land. It is so contrary to the Spirit of Christ. He is life, love, and light.

TAKE THE WATER "OUT THERE"

> *The Church is not just going to bring light to the world, but joy.*

What better life is there than joy?

There is going to be someone walking down the road, and they are going to say, "That guy is a Christian. Look how happy he is."

When was the last time that someone came to you and said, "I can see that you are a Christian because you are so full of joy."

Do you wake up in the morning saying, "Lord, how am I going to pay my bills? I have such a headache, and everyone is on my case. I guess I should just get on with the day."

How is that bringing life?

When you are on fire for God, and when His anointing is real in your life, you are so excited and happy. You just feel like you have to say something, do something, shout something, sing something or dance something because there is so much joy bubbling up out of you.

When was the last time that you felt that way about your salvation? That is a picture of what the Church will look like.

How? It is because you, as an apostle, would have done a good enough job that the fruit of the spirit is in every believer and that joy is going to be contagious.

Come on, who ever wanted to go and hang out with a bunch of people that are depressed? Sometimes, you go to certain church services and think, "Thank you, Lord, that I am not part of this bunch. I do not think that I can live a life like that. It seems terrible."

You do not have to frighten people by telling them they are going to Heaven or Hell. That has been beaten to death. Why don't we just bring some joy? We will see the body of Christ rise with such joy and life that anyone around us will catch it.

It will be so contagious because of that joy. Ezekiel goes on to say that the river started to get filled with lots of fish. There were big fish, little fish, ugly fish, and pretty fish. All the fisherman came, threw out their nets, and brought them in.

There is something about water. You do not need to tell a fish to be drawn to good water. It just goes there. However, the problem is that you have your little temple, where you are splashing in your little bathtub. Next to that, you have desert land. Beyond that, you have a sea.

You want those poor fish to flop through the desert and plop into your little bathtub, in your little temple. However, if you take the water to them, the fish will not be a problem.

If you want to reach the world and start getting the lost saved, then stop expecting them to do the big trek across the desert. You take the water to them.

When you are full of joy and life, and full of the Holy Spirit, those fish will say, "That water feels so good. Give me some more of that." There will be big fish, little fish, pretty fish, and ugly fish all around you.

Then, all you will need to do is cast a net. We will see in the End-Times a move of evangelism as we have never ever seen. There will be fish from every nation, every tribe, tongue, doctrine, denomination, and every last religion out there.

Can you see why the apostle has to have a pattern in place? Jesus spent three years with His disciples establishing that pattern before Peter stood up on the Day of Pentecost.

THE PATTERN

What would you do right now if three thousand people walked into your ministry? Would you know what to do with them? If not, you have not set up your pattern as an apostle because you should know what to do with them.

Peter knew what to do with them because Jesus had already laid the foundation and given them the structure. Before we see this move of God, this massive revival, the pattern has to be in place.

The pattern comes first. You cannot just be a typical expressive and wing it. You cannot wing this one. If you get that many people saved and have that type of effect, then you better be ready.

That is why God has pulled you aside for this season. It is so that you can get ready.

HEALING AND PROSPERITY

As the fish filled the river, trees started to grow on the side of the river for food and healing.

With that will come such an era of prosperity in the Church that they will lack for nothing. The rich among the people will entreat our favor. We will be above and not beneath, the head and not the tail.

The world will be coming to the local church for a loan, instead of the local bank.

"Lord, give me the money, and then I will walk in your anointing."

It does not work that way. We must build the temple first. Then, we will get the river flowing, and the rest will take care of itself. When we get to this stage, we will see every believer walking in the blessing of the Lord.

It will not just be financially, but in health and body. They will not have to find the next healing revivalist to be healed. They can go to any Christian and say, "Please pray for me. I am sick. Give me some of that tree of yours."

This is a natural result when the anointing flows. Those trees naturally pop up when the anointing is given its place in our lives. I do not think that any of us disagree with that. We want the anointing and the healing - but the temple comes first.

ARE YOU BUILDING THE TEMPLE?

You started with great zeal. You started to get this vision. I know that, even as I am sharing, you can pick out revelations that God has given you, patterns He has given you, and thoughts that have come to your mind.

You got so excited and were standing on the threshold of that time where the children of Israel had been in captivity for seventy long years and finally, overnight, something miraculous happened.

A new king, Persia, comes and conquers Babylon. He comes to the throne and sends a new decree to the land, "I am sending you back to build your temple." (Ezra 1).

"Not only am I going to allow you to return and build your temple, but I am going to fund it. Then, I am going to also give back everything that was stolen from it so that you can establish it."

As if that was not enough, he also said for them to go and ask their neighbors for goods and help, so that they could give them gifts along the way. They left loaded after coming stripped and scattered.

In an instant, a blink of an eye, God brought it altogether and gave them the desire of their heart.

YOUR JOURNEY TO YOUR APOSTOLIC MANDATE

Chapter 10 – Your Journey to Your Apostolic Mandate

Now, the call has gone out to you. You are much like these guys, Zerubbabel and Jeshua. Zerubbabel was the leader, and Jeshua was the High Priest. They got the call, and they were so excited, that they got everyone together.

They said, "Come on, guys, let's go build." They went singing and rejoicing. They were so pumped and excited. Then, they arrived at Jerusalem, and do you want to know what the first thing was that they built?

The Mandate Process

If you look at Ezra 3:2, you see that the first thing they built was the altar. Is that not the craziest thing? After getting all the way there, you would think that they would have built a few houses and a wall.

For me, I would build a bathroom and a kitchen first… but that is a woman thing.

The first thing they built was an altar. Before they did anything else, they began to sacrifice. When God calls you as an apostle, you spend what feels like seventy years in the wilderness, knowing God has called you and knowing that a time will come when the temple needs to be built and the work needs to be done.

It seems like forever that you are there. Then, one day, you get a knock at your door, and the door opens for you to walk through. Finally, you can begin to walk out the call that God has given you.

Perhaps you are placed into office, or some opportunity takes place, and you say, "Yes! Now is my time of visitation. All of this training, travailing, and waiting that I have gone through is over. Now is the time to go into the Promised Land that God has given."

First Up: Acquaintance with the Altar

Then, the first thing that you smack your face on is the altar. Instead of "glory hallelujah, external anointing and fire", you get "Die already!"

"Now that you are on the journey and pumped to start the call, I want you to give up your ideas and die to your opinion, and that root of temporal values must go. That bitterness is not acceptable. The vision that you had is dead, this character trait has to go, and that thing that you boast in must go. You must die."

The first thing that they instituted was daily sacrifices. You end up thinking, "Lord, this is the resurrection of my vision? This is me coming out of the wilderness? I am pumped and ready to go, and all I see is the altar in my face?"

It is the door that you have been waiting for. It is the very thing that you have asked for. You think, "I have finally been released to rise up as the apostle that God has called me to be."

Yes, you are. Now, flat on the altar is where you will start and where you will stay. That is where it begins and ends, because it is no longer I that lives, but Christ that lives in me. It is the beginning and end of our salvation (Gal 2:20).

It is like John the Baptist said, "May I decrease so that He may increase." That is why it begins with the altar, so that just in case there were a few visions there that you were still holding onto... they are gone now.

So, here is a word of advice. If you have any old visions, anointings or abilities, especially ministry - just let it go.

One time, I said to the Lord, "This anointing and ability that You have given me is something that You have given me."

He said, "That which is gold will remain, but that which can be shaken will be shaken, so that what cannot be shaken will remain." (Heb 12:27).

He told me to put those things that I had on the altar. So, every vision, anointing, and ability, you should just let it go. You know what is great about dying? Remember when I said that revival only comes to those that are dead?

Have you been crying for some revival? Why do you think that the first step is the altar? The first thing that they built was the altar. Then, just when you think that you cannot possibly let go anymore, the Lord says, "Now you are ready to start building."

You do so in fear and trembling because you know that you have nothing left to build with. You are so stripped and empty that all you can say is, "Lord, give me the pattern, and let me build what You want me to build."

However, you know that once you have finished building, it was not even you that could have done the building, because you were doing the impossible.

That was the point of all the death. You have to come to realize that God has called you to do something impossible.

If it was possible, you would have done it already. We would see it in the world already. However, God is calling you to do what He can do. He needs you to get into place. He has established this pattern since the beginning of time.

GET YOURSELF IN PLACE

He just needs to put you in the right place at the right time, and you just need to be the right vessel in the right place at the right time. Then, God will move. His plan will remain. If you think that this all depends on you, then you need to realize that His plan and pattern for His Church universal will remain.

He is simply giving you an opportunity to be the Zerubbabel and come and build it. However, if you do not want to, He will gladly pick up another, because His pattern will remain. It has been established since the foundation of the earth.

You just get yourself into place. To get yourself into place means that you need to knock off the pieces that do not fit. It is like a puzzle. If the piece does not fit, then it does not go with the picture.

God has a very clear place for you in His church, and a very clear part of the pattern that He needs you to build. So, you better become the kind of person that can fit that place. If you are not willing to, God will find another who is.

I am not just talking about salvation here. I am talking about building God's temple. You just need to do a little bit of studying in the Word to see that it had to be built to spec - down to the letter and millimeter. So, stop whining about the death and travail.

Do you not understand that God is shaping you to fit you into place?

You say, "More, Lord."

He strips you.

"Why, Lord?"

"You asked."

How did you think the "more" was going to come? If you were the kind of vessel that could fit "more" already, then you would already have it.

Every time His hand comes upon you to shape you, you should shout "Hallelujah! That hurt so good. God is shaping me to fit the place that I need to fill in order to establish this temple in His Church so that I can bring the glory and the fire. More, Lord. Shape me and change me."

It is like a woman in travail as she is in labor, crying out with each pain. Is she saying, "Stop?" No, she is saying, "More, more. Let's get this over with."

Do not whine when the altar is before you. The children of Israel did not whine. They ran to the altar and embraced it because they knew the power of the blood and of laying their sin aside. They knew what would happen after making their sacrifice. They knew the glory would come.

SECOND PHASE: TEMPTED BY THE WORLD'S WAY

Then, they started to build. You know what happened after that? A bunch of people had settled in the surrounding regions after the Israelites had been thrown out. Now these guys see the Israelites coming back and building their temple.

They start feeling antsy about it. They want to be part of the action, so they come in Ezra 4, "I can see that you guys are building the temple. We would love to help. We have all these resources and able-bodied men. We can do it double time.

Let's be a team and do an association. Why not sit down and make a treaty? Let's rub shoulders. You rub my back, and I rub yours. Let's work this out. You know, the more people that you know, the better it is for you.

In fact, I know who to refer you to in order to get you connected. Once you are connected, then you have the resources. The doors will open, and everything will happen for you. You can rise up overnight."

Ezra took one look and said, "I do not think so."

This is the first temptation that you are going to face when you start doing what God has called you to do. You are going to be tempted to compromise and do it the way that other people do.

"Don't you know that if you want to start a business in this day and age, the first thing that you need to do is get partners? You need to get people to support you, you need to go public, you need to get associations, and you need to get contacts."

> *That is the world's way of doing things. If this was*
> *possible, God would not have called you to do it.*

God does not call you to do what man does. He calls you to do what He does. If you think that all of your contacts and associations and who you know in this world are going to further your ministry, then you have not even begun to understand what an apostolic call is.

There is only one contact that I need, and He is Jesus Christ. It turns out that He knows a few people. However, Jesus is not good enough for us, is He? We need to know this pastor over there, this social site over here, and we have to do it the world's way, because that is the way that everyone else is growing their ministries.

If I want to get on TBN, this is what I need to do. You know guys, so far, I am not seeing a big temple with lots of water everywhere. If what has been done out there has not brought the Church into its glory yet, then how about you and I do something different?

How about you and I do only what God has told each of us to do? You build your piece of the pattern, and I will build my piece of the pattern according to the blueprint that God, the Father, has given me.

PRESSURE WILL COME

Let's raise up an End-Times Church that is built on the foundation of Jesus Christ and that is established with the fivefold ministry, one where every believer is walking in power and maturity. How about we do that rather?

That is "the impossible" that God has called us to do. No more compromise. The first thing you are going to get is pressure. Pressure from the church system, the world system, and your family and friends.

"Why rock the boat? You should do it the way that everyone else is doing it. This is the set way of doing things."

There are so many voices in your head, and after awhile, you think, "Am I being a little bit extreme? Am I perhaps being arrogant in thinking that what God told me is the right way, and their way is the wrong way?

Am I full of the flesh that I think that I can really do this thing on my own with only Jesus as my backing?"

You start to doubt yourself, and you start to wonder. It is good if you go through this process. You should travail and struggle through it.

Demos Shakarian, the founder of the Full Gospel Business Men's Fellowship, shared a fascinating story. He really had a burden for his vision. When he started it off, it died before it even got going.

There were about twelve to fourteen people. He was slogging through, and nobody wanted to come to these meetings. Eventually, he ended up hooking up with a gentleman who said, "Man, you have to come to the UK. The people will love you there.

You come over. I am going to arrange a meeting with all the pastors, and we are going to get you out there. I am going to use every contact that I have, and we are going to get your name out there and get this ministry started."

He thought, "Maybe this is the break that I have been looking for. Maybe I have been doing things the wrong way. Maybe me just trusting God alone, without using contacts, is foolish. Maybe I need to take advantage of this."

So, they spent all this money. They went on this big trip and toured Europe and did this whole thing. However, they did not get to hold one single meeting. The doors were shut in his face one after the other.

The Lord was giving a big, resounding "I don't think so!"

This happened more than once in his ministry. He tried to do it the typical way, the way that everyone else does it. Yet, every time that he did it, he hit his head against a wall. We thank God for that, because he was going through this process of compromise. He realized that there is a God way of doing things, and a worldly way of doing things. Today, his ministry continues to reach men all over the world with the gospel and has, in many ways, set the trend for men's ministry as we know it.

Not bad for starting with nothing, is it?

AFTER HAVING DONE ALL – STAND!

The problem is that you do not even get that it is the world's way until the world's way is suddenly swallowing your vision, and the fire in you is starting to dim.

You do not even know what God has called you to do anymore. It is time to get back to the original pattern, because that compromise has swallowed the fire that God has put in you. When you get that, it takes a moment to say, "I do not think so!"

Maybe I am arrogant, and maybe I am full of pride.

"God, you can strike me where I stand."

He is well able to bring me to death, and to crush me in the palm of His hand if I am out of line. However, as Apostle Paul said, "I must do not what man has told me to do, but what God has told me to do."

I will obey that. When you obey that, you will receive the same response that Paul received. They attacked him.

The same response that Ezra and Nehemiah got! This is what happens right after you make your big and bold, "I will not compromise" stand… you are attacked on every side.

So, they got hold of the king himself, sent off a letter, and started opposing everything that they were doing. People came there by force to stop them. In the end, all they got to do was lay a foundation.

They laid a foundation, and then the rest of the building stood. They said, "I know my vision was of God. I know that God brought me this far for a purpose, but I guess I was premature. Maybe it was not yet time. Perhaps I need to go back to the desert or continue with my day to day life."

If you are there, do not be discouraged. God is not done with you yet. You are called to build, and the door is about to open in front of you!

BUILD THE TEMPLE

CHAPTER 11 – BUILD THE TEMPLE

So, they built houses, established families, made the land nice and fruitful, and got on with life. All the while, the foundation of the temple laid bare for years and years, until one day, the prophet, Haggai, knocked on their door.

> **Haggai 1:3** *Then the word of the Lord came through the prophet Haggai:*
>
> *4 "Is it a time for you yourselves to be living in your paneled houses, while this house remains a ruin?"*
>
> *5 Now this is what the Lord Almighty says: "Give careful thought to your ways.*
>
> *6 You have planted much, but harvested little. You eat, but never have enough. You drink, but never have your fill. You put on clothes, but are not warm. You earn wages, only to put them in a purse with holes in it." (NIV)*

There was an emptiness in them. That is what happens when you compromise, when you come under so much attack and let your vision go and just get on with business. You think that you are building the work of God, that you are fulfilling your call, but all you are doing is building paneled houses.

You are saying, "Lord, bring the increase. Where are the finances? Why are our needs not met?"

When was the last time that you concentrated on building His temple, instead of your own house? Do not say that just because you have stood up to preach, written a few articles, or gone out and laid hands to heal a few folks that you have been building the temple.

No, that is just business as usual. What happened to the mandate, the vision, the fire, and doing the real stuff that God needs you to do? That is the problem with being in ministry. It is who we are and kind of like our job description most of the time.

You are doing your Sunday meetings, but when was the last time that you put a brick on the foundation that is going to remain from generation to generation? What happened to building the pattern that God wants you to build?

You are so busy building what everyone else wants you to build, what is comfortable for you to build, or even what you are capable in yourself to build.

> *Anybody can build a paneled house, but it takes the glory of God and a pattern from the Father Himself to build a temple.*

God started giving you that pattern, but you fell apart under all the pressure. You broke down and got discouraged. I do not condemn you for being discouraged, but I am saying that it is time to wake up.

You may have thought that you missed God or that it was just some stupid harebrained scheme, but now it is time to go back to the drawing board and realize that you need to set God's house in order.

There is this common saying, "I must get my house in order." That is great, but you have been spending too much time getting your house in order. It is now time to get God's house in order.

Here is the reality, if you are called to be an apostle, the condition of the Church as it is right now is upon your shoulders. Stop looking around and seeing what needs to be changed, and get out there and make the change.

Stop looking out there and judging who is doing it wrong when you are not even doing it right. Do not accuse others of building wrongly when you are not building at all. What sets you apart and separates you? What is the vision that God has given you?

If you want prosperity, want to see things going the right way, and are tired of the bag of holes in your ministry and life, then it is time that you start taking a good look at what you are building here.

Are you building God's temple, or are you building your paneled house? You have your stained glass windows, and everything looks nice, and you say, "We just expanded our building this week."

I do not care how many congregation members you have or how good of a speaker you are. Are you building the temple?

IS THE RIVER FLOWING?

Here is a good sign. Water starts to flow when the temple is built. Is the river flowing? Yet, you are waiting for the river to come and build your temple.

You say, "If revival comes, and the anointing comes, then my temple will come together. Everything will come right. I will suddenly get the pattern and know what to do."

No, it does not work that way. The Early Church, in the Day of Pentecost, was in the upper room praying. They had themselves in position, and then the anointing came. They already had the pattern. Then, the anointing came, and they walked the pattern out.

You need to get the pattern first and build the temple first, and then the anointing will come. You have it backwards.

"Lord, why have you not moved? You have given me so many promises. You said that the latter rain would be greater than the former rain. Lord, you promised me that your blessing would catch up with me and overtake me. Why is none of this happening?"

It is because you have not built the temple. All of this flows from the temple, not your paneled house. We are so busy making pretty and doing what is required of us and what we "need" to do, instead of what we should be doing.

A Word From God: Wake Up!

Haggai had to come and say, "Wake up!"

That is why we need the prophets in the Church today. They need to come and inspire the church of God to rise up and start building the Church, and to put each one in place. Together, the prophets and the apostles will get this temple built and established.

It said after that, that this was all Zerubbabel and Jeshua needed. They just needed someone to come and give them a good slap across the face a few times, and then they were ready.

They woke up and took some action. They sent a very good letter to the man who was governor at the time. They sent it to Persia and said, "According to what was originally said, it was decreed that we can go and build our temple."

They got wisdom from the Lord here, and they fought fire with fire. They said, "You go and see, and you will find that it was decreed and the first king signed that document saying that we could build our temple." (Ezra 5 and 6).

Then, this was released immediately. I asked myself, "Why was this not done years before? Why did they allow the temple to just sit there?"

You think, "Shame... they could not help it. They were stopped by force."

However, instead of fighting back, they said, "Oh well. Why did I think that I could do this? I may as well give up and get on with it. It is just too much work to push through. I am so tired of the opposition and of people speaking negatively against me.

I am tired of people pushing against me, and I am tired of the struggle. I am tired of having to beg, and of having to work so hard. Let me just do what I need to do, and get on with my life."

CONSIDER THIS YOUR HAGGAI CALL. "WAKE UP! IT IS TIME TO BUILD."

We could have been doing this years ago. However, you are waiting for God to do something. God has done something. He gave you the pattern. God will continue to do something as you continue to build it.

LEADERSHIP IS NECESSARY

Ezra 5 shows that they all got together, the prophets, Zerubbabel, Jeshua, and the high priests, and they started to build.

Just as it took Zerubbabel and Jeshua, Haggai and Zechariah, it will take the apostles and prophets to get the rest of the people in order. I love how it says that they sent the letter, and particularly these four started getting together and getting the people to start building again.

> *You see, it is up to the apostle. You are waiting for the people to get ready and to follow you. You need to get up and lead, and the people will follow. Get up and establish, and the people will build.*

It is for you, as the apostle, to take the lead. It is for you, as the apostle, to take action, to put your hand to the plow, to bring up the pattern that God has given you, and say, "You take that division, you build that wall, you are needed here to guard this family."

It is for you to get the show on the road. You are waiting for the people to be ready, and they were already ready years ago. If they are not ready, they will get ready quickly enough. They are waiting for you.

They are waiting for leadership. The minute these leaders jumped into action, the people were behind them. They were just waiting for someone to have the courage to stand up and do something about it.

WHAT ARE YOU GOING TO DO ABOUT IT?

We see a lot going on in the Church and in the world, and we all have these visions, especially as apostles, of what we know God wants to do. But what are you doing about it? Where are you putting your hand to the plow?

Listen, it is not just going to happen. You are not just going to wake up one day, and the new Church is upon us. God has always worked through the agency of man. Moses did not dream about the tabernacle, and then the next day it was just there when he woke up.

It was a process. He had to go and get the pattern, bring the pattern down, throw the pattern at the people, go back up and get the pattern again, come back down, and build the pattern. It was a process, a difficult process.

He also faced these same things. He was being pushed to compromise, and being attacked by those closest to him, but he pressed on and built that tabernacle.

Solomon did the same thing. He did not just wake up with gold everywhere. He had to do something about it. He had to take the pattern and actually build. When you build the temple, this pattern that God has given you, His glory will come.

Not only will God give you the wisdom to get the pattern. We will also continue in this book to speak more on the pattern and what it should look like, so that you can take a look at the blueprint that God has already given you and understand how to read it.

YOU ALREADY HAVE THE BLUEPRINT

God has given you a blueprint. You just do not understand the fullness of it sometimes. That is what I am shedding light on here. It is time for you to take that blueprint and start building according to His wisdom.

I cannot promise that you are going to get it right every time. That is why the altar is right there in the middle, because every time you add something wrong to that temple, the altar is at your face again. There is going to be sacrifice and death.

So, never forget that there is a reason why there was continual sacrifices and continual incense going up. There was a continual process.

Do you know when the deaths are the hardest for the apostle? It is not when he is going through preparation, or when he is going through training. The hardest deaths that an apostle ever faces are when he finally reaches office.

Preparation gets the materials ready for the altar, training builds the altar, and your office sees you lying on the altar. That is how I know when I am looking at someone who is called as an apostle.

They are not walking around saying, "Check out my temple." They are saying, "I know what my altar looks like from every angle."

They visit there daily, and it is like Paul said, "I die daily." It almost becomes their boast. Their boast is in how pathetic they are, and how they keep tripping over their own feet to the altar every day.

It is because they are not building this pattern by what they can do. They need something miraculous. This calling that we have is a miraculous calling.

I love what Haggai said to Zerubbabel. He said two things, and these are two promises that God is giving to you right now. He is saying to you, "If you will put down your compromise, take action, face the attacks and push through, the glory of the latter house will be greater than the former house, says the Lord. In this place, I will give peace."

You know that anointing that you had to die to, the ministry that you had to give up, the church that you were thrown out of, and the ministry that was stolen from you? These things are nothing. They are the former.

LET THE LATTER RAIN COME

The anointing, the vision, the wisdom and the revelation that God will give you when you are prepared to do it His way will be greater. However, He is not going to give it to you until you start putting your hand to the plow and start building.

"Lord, I am ready for that latter rain. Hit me."

Where is your temple? What are you going to do with all of that latter rain when it is splashing around? Where is it going to flow from? You do not have a temple. What is the pattern? Have you built it?

You are all ready to pray for the latter rain, but where is your temple? When you do build it and are ready to take action and be diligent, the Lord will say, "If you do your part, then I will do mine.

If you visit that altar, give up those gifts, abilities, people, ministries, bitterness, regret, your rights, and everything that you thought belonged to you, then I will give you greater things."

Is that not what Jesus said to Peter? He said, "We have given up everything - family, homes, brothers and sisters."

Jesus turned to him and said, "For everything that you have given up in this life, I will give you far more than what you have given up." (Luke 18:28).

However, you cannot hold onto the old and then say, "Lord, give me the new so that I can decide whether or not I want to let go of the old."

There is a season when you are on the altar, and you start to think to yourself, "Lord, never mind am I an apostle or am I called, I am barely hanging on to my salvation. Some days, I do not even feel like a Christian.

My anointing is gone. Suddenly, you take away my ability to preach. I am in the backside of the desert, and everyone is against me. The people that I thought would follow through with me have left, and I am all abandoned. What is going on? Am I wrong? Do I need to go back to the wilderness?"

No. Now that you have been stripped, it is time for action. Everything that the Lord has taken from you, He will restore one hundredfold. I can promise you that.

YOU ARE GOD'S SIGNET

I can also promise you this second beautiful promise,

> **Haggai 2:23** *'In that day,' says the Lord of hosts, 'I will take you, Zerubbabel My servant, the son of Shealtiel,' says the Lord, 'and will make you like a signet ring; for I have chosen you,' says the Lord of hosts."*

I will make you a signet, a gemstone that is my mark in this world. They would take a signet and make their mark on it. The Lord is going to take you, and you will be His mark on the Church.

You know how they brand cattle as ownership to show who the owner is? The Lord is going to take you, and you will be His signet so that when the world looks upon you they will say,

"He is God's! That is God's signet. That is His signature on you. I can see the Father. I can see the pattern. I can see the anointing. I can see the epitome of Christ right there. If I was looking for Jesus, that is His signet and His face."

He will raise you up as an example for many to follow, and kings will be drawn to the brightness of your rising. However, there is a price to pay. You cannot sit around waiting for someone else to do the job for you.

If God has given you a call, you are responsible before God to walk it out. It is time for you to take the load. It is time for you to motivate God's people. It is time for you to build God's Church.

STANDING IN THE EYE OF THE STORM

CHAPTER 12 – STANDING IN THE EYE OF THE STORM

> ***Exodus 19:16*** *Then it came to pass on the third day, in the morning, that there were thunderings and lightnings, and a thick cloud on the mountain; and the sound of the trumpet was very loud, so that all the people who were in the camp trembled.*
>
> *17 And Moses brought the people out of the camp to meet with God, and they stood at the foot of the mountain.*
>
> *18 Now Mount Sinai was completely in smoke, because the Lord descended upon it in fire. Its smoke ascended like the smoke of a furnace, and the whole mountain[a] quaked greatly.*

> ***Exodus 24:17*** *The sight of the glory of the Lord was like a consuming fire on the top of the mountain in the eyes of the children of Israel.*
>
> *18 So Moses went into the midst of the cloud and went up into the mountain. And Moses was on the mountain forty days and forty nights.*

When the Lord started indicating that my sole purpose was not to remain as a team member of my father's ministry, He showed me that there was going to be a change in my ministry.

I was quite comfortable. I was teaching the prophets, helping my father with the preaching, and even having people come for training. I thought that I was at the point where I was doing His work and fulfilling the mandate that I needed to fulfill.

Finally, after three years of intensive stress and struggle, I came to a place of rest. I thought that everything was good just the way it was. However, that was just the trial run.

Little did I know what the Lord really had in store for me. One time, I was going through an inner conflict and asked my dad to stand in prayer with me. As we prayed, I saw a storm, and I knew exactly what that meant.

I saw this mighty hurricane come, pick me up, and hurl me into the air. I did not know which side was up and which side was down. My hair was all over the place, so I could not even see where I was going, and my feet were off the ground.

Then the Lord said, "Stand in the storm of my grace and ride the winds of my mercy. Then, you will be lifted up and carried into my perfect will."

Your Comfort Zone is Shaken

I saw this storm carry me to the place where He wanted me, and then my feet landed. From the time that I had that vision, all hell broke loose in my life. It was turned upside down. The nice comfort zone that I had found was suddenly changed.

The Lord indicated that this place was no longer where I belonged. He wanted to send me out.

"I know that you are comfortable in this group and family, but I am plucking you out and taking you somewhere else. If you would just stop kicking and screaming for a minute, you might see My will within the storm."

There came a metamorphosis in my life, a changing of learning to stand in the eye of the storm.

I had to come to the place of surrendering myself to the winds that buffeted me. When I could surrender to the circumstances and change that I felt was unfair accusation and struggles, and everyone standing against me, this was when His glory came.

That was when He picked me up and showed me the full vision that He had for me. I just had a taste. I thought I knew.

I had become too comfortable. Until I was willing to go through that storm and stand in the eye, the Lord was not able to give me the full picture. Then, He could show me where I was meant to go.

> *It is not comfortable to stand in a storm. However, when you stand in the eye of the storm, there is peace. It is in the eye of the storm that you will find the glory of God.*

That is what Moses found when he climbed the mount in the scripture that I shared above.

CALLED TO CLIMB THE MOUNTAIN

Moses went into the middle of the cloud and climbed up in the mountain.

In this chapter, I want you to climb the mount with me. Come and stand in the eye of the storm. This is what you have been looking for. You have been kicking and screaming and shouting about how unfair this is.

"Why does this have to be so difficult for me?"

"Why do I have to face so many conflicts?"

"Why do I have to be so emotional?"

"Why can I not just be like everyone else?"

You are struggling, but it is time to stand in the eye of the storm and let it carry you. You need to let it buffet you and carry you wherever God wills it.

At this stage in the game, I hate to break it to you, but you gave your control up to the heavenly Father. You do not have it anymore. You do not possess that control anymore. You signed on the dotted line for boot camp.

You signed those papers, and from the time you said, "Yes and amen", the Lord started doing a work. Whether you kick and scream, or chill out and let the Lord have His way, you are still going to get there.

Whether you get there with bumps and bruises or with the glory is up to you. How many times do you have to fall flat on your face before you figure out that you are doing something wrong?

It's time to submit yourself to the will of God. I went through a terrible time of struggling. There were even times when I said, "That's it! I do not want this anymore. Take it away. I give up!"

"Take me off the list. What am I doing this for? This is just for nothing. I am wasting my time."

After that, I was sure that the Lord would say, "Alright, write her off!"

GOD'S GOT THIS

At the end of the day, you are really not in control. The Lord is in control of your calling. No matter how many times you fail, if your heart remains turned to God and open, He will always raise you up.

It may take you longer to get there, but God will never stop moving upon you and changing you. He will never stop calling you to stand in His cloud, to stand upon the mountain in the eye of His storm.

It is there that you will see Jesus face-to-face. It is there that you will hear His heartbeat and His word to you.

Do you want to know why you have to go through so much death? Do you want to know why the Lord continues to bring the chisel and the cross to your life?

It is because you keep moving away from that place within the eye of the storm. If you would just remain there, the deaths and chisel blows would not need to come. You would already hear from the Lord for yourself.

Us expressive types always run off in seven different directions all at once. We get so excited and emotional.

The Lord started sharing an idea with me once, a concept for ministry, and I said, "That is so awesome!" Then, I ran off into so many directions, trying to make it work. I fell flat on my face.

As I was running around, the Lord was trying to get through to me.

"I was not finished talking to you yet."

I was so busy running and doing my thing. He eventually just sat down and waited for me to wear myself out.

Then, when I came crawling back to Him, He said, "Are you finished because I never got to finish telling you what I had in mind? If you would sit still for long enough and listen, then you would get the full picture."

Every time we step out of that, we get into trouble. If we would just remain in that place where we can hear His voice, then we would not need to fall flat on our face all the time. The Lord does not glorify in our death and rejoice in our humbling. He wants to raise us up.

We bring the humbling upon ourselves because we are off doing our own thing.

STARTING THE CLIMB

What will you see when you climb up the mountain and come into the eye of the storm? When you stand in the pillar of fire and the cloud of smoke, what will you see?

THE FACE OF THE LORD

You will see the face of the Lord, instead of your flesh. I was really going through a struggle with so many issues. I was listing all my failures and issues.

The Lord said, "If you had more faith in My strength than in your weakness, then I could do something with you."

> *We are so busy looking at ourselves, and our own*
> *weaknesses and inabilities, that we do not see His*
> *ability. If you just had as much faith for what God*
> *can do as you do for what you cannot do, you*
> *would change nations.*

Our faith in our weaknesses is greater than our faith in God. Our faith in our inability is stronger than our faith in God's ability. Our faith in our lack is greater than our faith in His abundance.

Why is it that we always hold onto the things that drag us down like anchors? When you come to the place where you are in the eye of the storm, what is the mirror that you are going to see?

It is not going to be you because you are going to be surrounded by the hurricane. No matter where you look, whether left or right, you are going to see Jesus. When you are surrounded by the storm, you cannot see anything else.

You are upside down, back to front, and the wind is blowing and howling. You cannot see out, and no one else can see in. You can only see what God can do, what He is capable of doing, and what the possibilities are.

You can see His vision and mandate for you. You can see the whole world that is before you.

When the power of God comes upon you, you think, "Let me at 'em!"

When the power of God came upon Samson, he took the gates of the city and carried them up a mountain. That is the power of God. Elijah outran a chariot when the power of God came upon him.

The power of God brings us way beyond anything that our human bodies are capable of doing. Anything is possible within that storm.

WITHOUT THE POWER YOU ARE... WELL... POWERLESS

When you stand in His glory and power, you can say, "Mountain, be uprooted and cast into the sea. Valley, rise up. River, pour forth."

However, we are so busy trying to do these things with our own works and principles.

"I have studied your books and the prophetic and apostolic courses. I know all the principles. I have them all in my head."

Those principles were to do one thing for you. They were meant to get you into the eye of the storm, where you could then be empowered to apply those principles. Without that empowerment, you are empty. You are nothing but a little pop gun.

You can have principles from Apostle Paul to Spurgeon, and you can have your head filled with knowledge. You can even have the full pattern of the Church, the full pattern for the tabernacle, point by point.

However, until you have the empowerment of the Holy Spirit, you are an empty vessel. Your work means nothing. Even the logos word is dead, until it is empowered by the Spirit when it comes up as rhema out of your spirit.

Until you have that, you have not even begun.

It is not enough to have principles and to know, feel, and desire. What you need is the glory of God in your life.

Then, you need to reflect that glory to everyone out there.

THE GLORY

When you come to that point where you have studied everything and done absolutely everything and are still nowhere, then you need to ask yourself the question, "What am I missing?"

I will tell you what's missing. The glory of God is missing. You are an empty vessel.

I do not care how clever you are or how much you know, or if you are on the cutting edge of what is going on in the prophetic and apostolic movement. Do you have the glory of God in your life?

Are you standing within the storm, and are you hearing His voice? Most importantly, are you reflecting that glory to God's people?

What is the use of all this stuff if you are not being empowered to apply it?

Are people noticing it on you? When you walk into a room, do people see it, notice it, and want it?

Do you want to know who God raises up?

Look around you. It is the stupid people. Do you know why evangelists move so powerfully and why they do not go past evangelism? It is because they do not stop long enough to figure it out.

They are not trying to understand it. They just stand there saying, "Ok, let's do this!"

God could even use a fisherman. When we are so filled with "trying to understand", we miss His purpose.

It takes someone like Paul, who had both. This is where you fall into place. You have the knowledge, wisdom, and principles. Yet, you are missing the glory. If you put the two together, you have someone who can spearhead the apostolic movement.

You cannot have either or. You need both. We get these prophetic types who lean to the glory side, praise and worship, power, and glory, but when it comes to principles, they cannot really change people's lives and take them to the next level.

They just keep pouring water on people's heads. People are thinking, "I am really hungry. I would like some bread. I would like you to teach me how to do this."

They just pour water until people are soaked, which is fine for a couple of meetings. However, this guy has to go home. What change are you bringing to the body of Christ universally?

It is not enough to be on either side. It is not enough to just have glory and revival. I am all for having revivals, but that is not enough. That is all fluff. You do not have the principles to add to that.

WHERE IS YOUR MAP?

What map are you going to give people to live their lives by? It is not enough to just give them the anointing and say, "Go home!"

When they go home, they have problems. They have a family, trouble at work, and financial difficulties. They need principles.

Imagine that they come to you, and you give them the principles and empower them by the Holy Spirit and then send them forth. That is a bit like Samson taking a couple foxes and tying their tails together, putting fire in them, and sending them out into the enemy's camp.

Some of us are too busy teaching the foxes how to run. On the other hand, we are burning the foxes. We need to give them both. We need to tie their tails together, give them direction, and *then* set them on fire.

This is a whole new level, the level that God wants to take you to. It is called climbing the mountain.

EXPERIENCING GOD IN HIS FULLNESS

What you will experience on top of that mountain is God in His fullness.

Have you been looking for the next level?

Even now in the Spirit, I see those that have been running and tasting a bit of this and that. It's like a having a craving, but you do not know what the craving is for. You can just taste something in your mouth, but you do not know what it is.

You will only know what you want once you have tasted it and realize that this is it. When you come into the eye of the storm, it will be what you have been craving. You will experience God in His fullness, in the full Trinity.

You will come to experience the gentle breeze of Jesus, the love anointing, the flow that comes up from within and causes you to bubble up with emotion. You will see Him face-to-face. You will experience and hear His heart.

You will come to that intimate secret place, and you will also experience the mighty rushing wind of the Spirit of God. It will come upon you, change you and conform you, and the winds will blow and toss you in the air.

You will also experience the thunder of the voice of God. You will come to experience His conviction. You will know His hatred for sin and for the work of the enemy in His church.

Most people lean on one of those. They emphasize the move of the Spirit, the need to live a righteous life, or they emphasize the love and intimacy with Jesus. Each one of these is powerful in itself.

THE NATURE OF THE TRINITY

However, if you take all three of them and put them into a triple-braided cord, you will have the apostolic movement. The body of

Christ will experience God in His fullness. What part have you experienced?

Whichever part you have not experienced is the part that you need to be seeking God for. You need to know God in His fullness.

When Craig and I were dating, he was a great guy with a good sense of humor. However, when we married, there was a greater sense of intimacy, and I learned more about him.

After having a couple of children, I even learned more about him. I continue learning different aspects of his personality. There are different skills that he has, and even now, I am still learning likes and dislikes that he has.

There are so many parts of his personality that I am learning now that I did not know when we first met. I just thought he was pretty cool.

As our relationship evolves, I continue to get to know different sides of him. As we face different situations together, and I see him respond in different ways, I think, "I never knew he could do that. I never knew that was in him."

IT GETS DEEPER

It is the same with the Lord. You think you know the Lord.

"I know the Lord. I love Him, and I know that He loves me."

However, there needs to come an evolution where you get to know all the sides of His personality. You need to know every aspect of Him, in the entire Trinity. This is the problem in all the moves that have come before us – they have all emphasized on one side of the Lord.

Now, they are great. Each one brought massive revival. Yet, there is a new move coming to the Church that is going to take all of these things and bring them together into one glorious, consuming fire.

It starts with you and I today.

When I talked to the Lord before writing this book, He said to me, "At these great revivals, hundreds and thousands of people come, and they all get touched. You have heard the stories of how pastors go and get a touch and take it back to their churches.

Now, the problem with that is that the ministers are so busy dealing with the masses that they do not take the time to spend with those pastors that are going to go back and reach their entire congregation.

I will bring you a select few people that I have hand-picked, and they will bring thousands of people with them. When they come, they are going to receive what I am giving you to give them, and then they are going to take it out and give it to everyone else."

You are the one that is going to go out there and do that work. You are going to take what God has for you. Everyone is unique and will implement it differently, but you will take a fire with you that is going to touch the nations.

That is our mandate. We take the leaders, those that God has chosen, and give that to them and let them go out. Let's go raise the sleeping giant. That is what you are called to do.

You are not reading this book by mistake.

The work is vast, but the Lord will empower you to do it. You will find that empowerment in the eye of His storm.

The Apostolic Mandate

PREPARED FOR GREATNESS

CHAPTER 13 – PREPARED FOR GREATNESS

> *2 Corinthians 3:18 But we all, with unveiled face, beholding as in a mirror the glory of the Lord, are being transformed into the same image from glory to glory, just as by the Spirit of the Lord.*

Before you can see Jesus face-to-face and come to that place of glory, there needs to be a bit of stripping. We live in a society where it is almost a necessity for survival to put up walls that show that we have it together.

We want people to know that we have everything in control and that we see what is going on. I see people walking around with this attitude all the time. I think, "You so do *not* have it all together."

We all can see right through that.

However, you put up walls saying, "I have it together. I am good at this. I can handle this."

The truth though is that you do not have it together, and you do not have it under control. Even if you do have control, you still have a problem because God should have that control.

The first thing that needs to come is a removal of those veils, preconceived ideas, and wrong motives. Even the wrong motives are not as bad as the veils and the covering of our hearts.

If we cannot even open our hearts to one another, how are we going to open our hearts to God? How will He reflect Himself through us? Where do you think He is going to shine through if you are a closed vessel that does not have an outpouring?

WHAT TO DO WITH THE "MORE"

What is He going to do? Is He just going to keep filling you? Where is your exit point?

You keep saying, "More, Lord. More, Lord."

What are you going to do with it once you have it? Where are you going to pour it out?

If you cannot even get a breakthrough in praise and worship or with fellow brothers and sisters, how are you going to raise up nations and change the lives of people?

"It is easy. I will just stand behind the pulpit, and the Lord will do it."

You are the vessel. The buck stops with you. If God is going to move, He is going to move through you. You are not going to stand in one place, and the Lord moves in another place. That is not how it works.

He needs a vessel. Yet, you have all these walls and veils, and your heart is so tightly shut up that no one can get in. God cannot get in there either. If He cannot get in, then He cannot get out. If He cannot get out, then He cannot use you.

So, the first things that need to go are the veils, walls, and the "I have it together" attitude. Perhaps, it is time to admit that you do not have it together. Maybe you need to let down the guard and say, "Lord, I am a mess, and I actually cannot do this."

FACING SOME HARSH REALITIES

Yet, you try so hard. Perhaps you had a father that expected a lot of you. You are trying to live up to these expectations, and you are always falling short. You come to a place where you think you have it together, and you can do it.

That is called striving, and that has to go. You are so busy running in seven directions that you are missing God. He is right there waiting for you to come and just sit down with Him.

However, you are striving, trying, and pushing. When that is the image that you are looking at, you will find that you will never attain. You have this image of what you need to be, and you never get there.

One of two things happen. You either become religious or conceited and put up masks but are empty inside, or you go into the world. That is a religious veil that has to go.

The only expectation that God has for you is that you stand in the storm and allow yourself to be buffeted by the wind a bit. He does not expect you to be anything because He will make you into that something that you need to be.

You are so busy trying to make yourself into this image and vessel, and He has a whole different plan for you. He is saying, "Would you get finished so that I can actually do something with you?"

I had this shocking dream once. I dreamed that I was a pot, and I got smashed. When I woke up, I knew what was coming.

The Lord said, "The season is over for the image that you were; it is time to be something else."

SHAPED BY HIS HAND

He fashioned me by His hand. You cannot fashion yourself. I never saw a pot jump onto the potter's wheel and start fashioning itself. It does not put a dent here and a handle there.

It needs the hand of the potter to shape it. The hand of the potter is Jesus. For too long, you have been trying to put on your own handles. You are going to come out looking strange. Let Him do the work. He is more capable than you are.

All you need to do is surrender yourself to the storm. He will do the rest. When He wants you to speak, He will put you on the ground, and He will empower you. The rest of the time, you think, "I am so dead and un-anointed."

Then suddenly, He picks you up, puts you in place, and the power comes upon you. You think, "Where did that come from?" It came from Him because He did it. It is really all about Him.

I wrote a song that says, "Come and stand within my fire. Do you really want to see the nations? The shaking will come, but not because of you. It will come because of Him."

Pity we just do not have more faith in Him than in our own ability to fashion ourselves into what we think He wants. We have these images of what we think God wants.

You are not God. You do not know what is in His mind. You do not know the picture that He has, so why don't you just let it go for a bit and let Him do the work? Let Him fashion you, shape you, and take the veils away.

Let go of the striving, trying, and the preconceived ideas. Stop closing your heart, and lay yourself bare. It's time for a funeral – your funeral.

LETTING THE OLD PASS AWAY

Everything that was before you read this, it is no more. It is over and dead. This is a new road for you. Everything that you had, earned, achieved, or thought you wanted is no more from this day forward. It is gone.

From this day, the Lord is taking you back down to the foundation, and He will build upon it.

He is going to build His mandate and pattern for your life. It is time to let go of the old because it has some holes in it. You are like a leaking pot. He wants to refashion you. Let the old go. I mean it. It is over. Let it go!

It is going to take you a couple of days to fully understand what God is saying to you right now. Do not think that you are the only one that this message is for.

The Lord has been telling us that things are not going to be the same. Before writing this book, and after writing this book, things are going to change. He is doing a very specifically timed work.

Before this book, and while reading it, the Lord has called everything to death, wiped everything away. Afterwards, He is going to start a new building, shaping, and fashioning of the image and vessel you are.

He wants to make you into His vessel of glory. It is not all about death, but it is about glory and coming to stand in the eye of His storm. Everything that you did before now, you did outside of the full knowledge.

It is strange how when you first get a revelation, you feel like this is the full thing. But then a couple months down the line, the Lord adds more, and you feel like you did not know anything.

THE PROGRESSIVE REVELATION

There was a time when we preached five messages on the prophetic and thought that was it. We thought this was the entire message on the prophetic. However, the Lord gave me no less than 9 full books on the subject (and still counting...).

When I added the final word to the last book of the *Prophetic Field Guide Series*, I thought, "I have hardly touched the surface about what a prophet is."

I thought the same about the *The Moses Mandate*, in the apostolic. Originally, we thought he was the only apostolic type. As we continued to run on that track, the Lord told us that we only had one part of the picture.

We thought that we had the picture already. We are pretty arrogant. I have not met an apostle yet who is not a little arrogant, at least when they first start out. (So yeah... you are not alone.)

We thought that we had the answer and that we knew all there was to know. As the Lord started unfolding more revelation, I realized that we did not know anything. Now the more He teaches me about the prophetic and apostolic, the more I feel like I am sneaking a peek into a forest and have only just comprehended the first tree I saw.

It is the same with you. The Lord has given you one piece. Moses went up the mountain a few times before he got the full pattern. He did not go up once and have a glory hallelujah time and take the people into the Promised Land.

He went up several times. Each time, the Lord gave him more of the pattern. If you are not familiar with this, I cover it in the chapter "Climbing the Mountain" in *The Moses Mandate* book.

As you read it, you will see how I share about how he goes up a couple of times. Only on his last visit does he see the glory of God and come down shining. It is a progression. The Lord showed it to him bit by bit.

If you are so arrogant to think that you have the entire picture of your mandate and that you know what God wants to do, then you have not seen anything yet. You have not even started. The tiny picture that you see is not anything.

A Change of Perspective

I remember when we stayed on the coast and saw what appeared to be this big mountain out in the ocean every morning. We called it "The Disappearing Island" because some days you could see it, and some days you could not, due to the mist.

After a couple of years, we moved. I discovered that the one mountain was actually three islands. However, where we were staying, we could only see this one, big island. When we moved and saw it from another perspective, we actually saw how big it really was.

We look at revelation that way. We see this one thing, but when God starts to move us around a bit, we see things that we have never seen before. So, do not think that you have begun to see what God is going to do in your life. Do not think that you have your plan, and it is ready to be set in motion. You have not begun to understand. Only when you are in office will you even start to get the full picture.

If you think that you have the full picture now, it is time for you to die again because you do not. Until you can let that go and say, "Ok, Lord, show me what You want me to see," then you are going to be stuck with that small portion.

If you are happy with that, good for you. Stick with your portion. The Lord will bless you in that portion. However, you will never know what is on the other side of that mountain. If you would just let go of this viewpoint a bit and leave yourself aside, maybe you will start to get a picture of what God really has in store for you.

REFLECTING CHRIST

The next major change that will take place in your life is that others will look at you and see God, not you.

In this Church age, it has become quite fashionable to be the superstar. Everyone wants to be seen. When you can come to that place of standing in His storm, you cannot see the people, and they cannot see you.

They will see God around you. That is what they are drawn to and what they will want. This is what they will be touched by.

What are you striving for in ministry? Why do you want to be an apostle?

When you see yourself ministering in five or ten years, what do you see yourself doing? Why do you see yourself doing that?

What are the people going to see when you stand up there? Are they going to see you or Jesus Christ?

When you come to the place of standing in the eye of His storm, that is when they will see Jesus. Jesus said that we must go into all the world and preach the gospel. We are to be His messengers and reflect Him to His people.

However, if we are so busy reflecting ourselves, how are they going to get to see Jesus? There is one thing that I really cannot handle. It is when I have someone come to me and tell me about all the wonderful exploits that they have done for God.

"I healed countless people. When I prayed, gold was manifest on people's hands. I was invited to preach at this big event, and everyone raved about my message."

Curious... what did God do at these meetings?

God will even use you because you have faith. The gifts and callings of God are irrevocable. You can get your portion and be happy with that, but I want the glory. The gifts are not enough for me.

If you want the glory, you must be prepared to sacrifice yourself for Christ. When you tell people what you are doing in ministry, what are you telling them?

Are you telling them your accomplishments and how successful you are?

What is God doing in your ministry and in your life? I do not want to know what you are doing. I want to know what God is doing. I want to see Jesus.

Consider this. If you speak to any worldly businessman or superstar out in the world, they are going to tell you, "I starred in this show, I wrote this song, and I made a huge impact in the market."

HIS GLORY SETS YOU APART

So, what makes you any different? What is going to make you the light that the nations are going to flock to?

Is it how good you are, accomplished you are, and how magnificent you are?

They are going to Hollywood for that. That does not take any anointing. What makes you different is the power and glory of God. That is what it will take to set the body of Christ as a city set upon a hill.

This will bring the empowerment and glory of God. They will look at you and see Jesus and not just another big shot or superstar. They do not need to see another great preacher, but a very ordinary person with an extraordinary Jesus.

This is what it is about.

Sometimes, it is a bit difficult to separate your own ambitions from the ambitions of God. However, none of the disciples started with the right motivation either. Yet, when the Lord was finished with them, they sure had the right motivation.

When the Lord was finished with them, they laid a foundation for the New Testament Church.

God is calling you to lay a foundation for the End-Times Church. This is not one small portion or the call to just one death. This is not just a small vision.

It is not enough to be ordinary, to be like everyone else. It takes no ability to strive, make the contacts, or get in with the right people.

In all these great revivals, people go home and get on with their normal, daily lives. I hate to break it to you, but that is what happens.

You hear of those revivals of the past where they had those huge tent meetings. Thousands of people were healed in these things. What remains of them today?

The stories that they told are all that remain.

Where is the foundation, the End-Times Church, the glory of God in every believer?

They just went away saying, "I was healed. Praise God."

"I fell under the power. Praise God. It was glorious. Let's go back next week for more!"

Where is the glory and the power in the Church? How is the church going to get the power unless you impart it to them and release it over them?

It is not enough to just have revival. It is not enough to be a fancy preacher. Are you changing lives?

THE LIFE CHANGER

The only way that you are going to change lives is if you reflect Jesus. He is the life changer around here. When I look around and see some of those that have been with us for a while, I see changed lives. I think, "That's Jesus!"

There may only be a handful, but Jesus took twelve disciples. There were hundreds that flocked to Him. They came for a touch of His glory. They wanted to touch the hem of His garment.

They were healed, and multitudes were fed, but only twelve remained to lay the foundation. It was those twelve who started the movement.

What made them different from the masses that knew Jesus?

Jesus had seventy disciples other than the twelve. He imparted His anointing to them. They went in and healed the sick in the neighboring cities. It was not just the twelve who performed those miracles.

What made the twelve different?

They received that impartation and empowerment directly from Jesus, and they went out and changed lives.

If you want to be a superstar, then lay down a heritage that will withstand generation after generation. When you and I are gone, what will remain? Who will remember your anointing and glory?

> *No one is going to remember your name or how great and wonderful you are. They will remember Jesus. He remains, and His is the foundation of the Church.*

We are so busy running after these dreams and trying to get big. Yet, Jesus is already big. We just need to step into Him.

Why are you trying to build yourself up when He has already "arrived"?

Just stand in the eye of the storm. If you want to see changed lives, it will take more than some fluff and a bit of teaching. It is going to take a commitment from you, empowerment from the Holy Spirit, and for you to follow it through.

THE PROOF OF YOUR CALL

CHAPTER 14 – THE PROOF OF YOUR CALL

> **Deuteronomy 9:5** *It is not because of your righteousness or the uprightness of your heart that you go in to possess their land, but because of the wickedness of these nations that the Lord your God drives them out from before you, and that He may fulfill the word which the Lord swore to your fathers, to Abraham, Isaac, and Jacob.*

How righteous are you today?

The Lord does not care.

> **It is not by your righteousness that He has called you, but by their unrighteousness. It is not by your ability that He has called you, but because of their hunger.**

When was Moses sent to deliver the children of Israel? Was it when he felt like doing it, and he killed the Egyptian and landed himself into trouble?

He was full of zeal, ready to run off and deliver the Israelites. He was the savior.

That did not work out well for him. It landed him forty years in the wilderness. Have you been there yourself?

When did God send Moses to the children of Israel?

The Word says

> **Exodus 3:9** *Now therefore, behold, the cry of the children of Israel has come to Me, and I have also seen the oppression with which the Egyptians oppress them.*

God heard the cry of the children of Israel and sent them a deliverer. God did not raise up Moses because he was so wonderful, but because of the cry of His people.

The Lord has not raised you up because you are more righteous than the rest.

I said to some team members once, "Do you really want to know why God is using you? It is because you are the most foolish, weak vessel that He could find."

God is glorified in our weakness. He delights in taking the weak and foolish things of this world. What use is it to take someone who is successful and use them?

People looking at how God uses you will say, "They had that in them all the time." However, we know the truth. We all know where God found us. We know His strength was not shown through our talent, but rather through our weakness.

God takes the most pathetic losers that He can find, and He raises them up so that when they are raised up, He gets the glory.

So, is it by your righteousness and abilities that you were called to be an apostle?

No. We are a bunch of losers. Welcome to the club. It is a good place to be. That is what qualifies you.

HE ANSWERS THE CRIES OF HIS PEOPLE

This is why he is going to raise you up and use you. He is going to use you because His people cry out to Him day and night, and they are saying, "Send us a deliverer."

Go into any church, speak to any believer, and what is the cry of their heart? It is, "Lord, I need change. I want to see your face. Lord, I need you to set me free."

There is a hunger in the Church, even now. There is a massive hunger in the Church in every believer. Whether they are voicing it or not, they are looking for something different.

A prophet rises up, and everybody rushes to him because they think that he has the thing that they have been hungering for.

They go to prophetic revival after prophetic revival to be prophesied over, countless times.

It is because they are looking for that something that they can taste, but they can never find it. So, they just go to revival after revival and prophetic meeting after prophetic meeting to get more and more.

They are never satisfied because they are not given something tangible. God has heard their cries, and His heart is stirred towards them. So, He raises us up. He has raised us up because of their cry and hunger.

He has raised us up because of the unrighteousness of this world. When we look around us and see the sin and the decadence, that is why He has raised us up. It is not because of our righteousness, but because of their unrighteousness.

We are going to take this land for Jesus, and it is not because we are so powerful and mighty. It is because they are so unrighteous, and He wants to prove Himself to them.

YOU WERE SENT BECAUSE OF THE UNJUST

I was reading through Judges and Kings. You see how they really messed things up when they did things by themselves. King Ahab was a pretty bad king, but there was a time when the enemy came against him in the valley.

Ben-Hadad said, "Their God is only the God of the valleys. So, I am going to attack them in a different area. I will prove myself, and we will overcome Israel." (1 Kings 20)

God sent a prophet to Ahab and said, "You will win this war because they have said that I am only the God of the valleys, and they can defeat you elsewhere. I am going to prove myself to these people and show them that I am the God of the whole world."

He took a sinful king, who worshipped idols and was into demon worship, and gave him the victory over the enemy.

Was it because of his righteousness?

I think not. It was because of the enemy's unrighteousness and the fact that they dared to defy God. God will even use a sinful man to shine forth his glory.

It was because of God's people's hunger that He is raising you up. We have proved this time and time again. We have said to someone, "What do you want from God? How hungry are you? If you are hungry, you will get it."

If I get no revelation and nothing comes out of me, then you did not ask. Prophets are not like psychics who just get into the realm of the spirit.

God will give you what you want through me. However, the Lord will only give it, if you want it. Your faith draws it out of a willing vessel. As others come to you, you will find yourself moving in ways that you never did before.

Have you suddenly found yourself moving in healing and thought, "I do not even have the gift of healing?"

Do you know why that is happening? It is not because of "your healing gift", how wonderful you are, or your prophetic gifts. They were so hungry that they clung to the hem of your garments and said, "God, you have to touch me. Please Lord, just one drop from you."

God looked at you and said, "There is a vessel that I can use to touch My child with."

He releases through you, and that person's need is met. It has nothing to do with your righteousness or ability. It was because of their hunger and cry to God.

John G. Lake shared a time when he was really sick and was on medication. He said, "I have to get to one of Dowie's meetings because I know that if I get there, God will heal me."

He put aside his medication and pushed his way there. When he got there, he could not get to Dowie. So, he got a hold of a deacon and said, "Pray with me!"

When the deacon prayed, the power of God came. John G. Lake was healed, set free, and delivered. He went home glorifying God.

The deacon shook his head and said, "In all of the twenty years that I served God, I never had that happen in my ministry."

It never happened again after that either. It was John's faith that released what was in that man.

POWER ON TAP

> *We can have all of the power of God contained within us, but until someone comes to draw it out, like the woman who touched the hem of Jesus' garment, it is not going to come out.*

You see, Jesus was full of the anointing. All she needed to do was take it from Him. Jesus did not heal anyone in His own hometown, except a few sick. It is because they had no faith to draw it out of Him. It is their hunger that will draw it out of you.

There is a pressure when you look at the big names out there, and they are moving in signs and wonders and seem so magnificent.

You think, "If people do not fall or get healed, I am not as good as those big names."

Maybe you are just ministering to the wrong people, because it is their hunger that will draw it out of you. If someone needs to be touched from God, and they cry out, He will give them a visitation. In addition, does it occur to you that God desires to use you in a different way?

If everyone was ministering that way, who would heal the brokenhearted or set at liberty those who are oppressed by the devil?

God hears the cry of the elect. He will answer those cries through you, and all you need to do is stand in the eye of the storm and be obedient.

You need to hear His voice and know where to go. Then, His hand will move you. He will pick you up, and He will carry you where you need to go. You just need to stand in that place.

YOUR FIRST STEP TO THE MOUNTAIN TOP

You need to put everything down because you are going to be climbing the mountain. When you take Jesus' hand and look into His eyes, He will pull you up the mountain.

When you can let go of all of you and look at all of Him, you are going to start moving up the mountain. There will come a time when you look around you and think, "Oh my, I am here." You will not even know how you got there.

You would have been so captured in the gaze of Jesus that you would not have known where you were going.

It is strange, but the journey goes so much quicker that way. However, do you know what you have been doing?

You are like the children of Israel who have been walking around the mountain for forty years. The Lord is saying, "I am up here. You are missing something."

Jesus knows the way. He is the way. If you look upon Him, put your head to His chest, hear His voice to you, and develop that relationship, you will hear Him say, "Move here. Go there."

You will come to the place where you will know Him in His fullness. Yet, it all starts with looking in the eyes of Jesus.

The Lord is bringing you to this first step. This is where you need to start. You will come to that storm and that pillar of fire soon enough. However, you need to start by looking in the eyes of Jesus.

You cannot look in the eyes of your abilities and accomplishments. You cannot look in the eyes of "what will man think" or "that is what everyone else is doing, so we should do the same."

Have you asked God what to do? What has He said to you today? What did He say to you yesterday?

You should be hearing His voice all the time.

You cannot say, "The Lord gave me this revelation twenty years ago."

That is a bit stale now. What did He tell you this morning? What are you living right now?

You should be in constant communion with Jesus all the time. When you are meeting people and walking around, you should be hearing His voice continually.

Are you there yet? Is His voice that clear to you?

If not, that is your starting point.

The call has come to you to step into the fire and stand in the eye of the storm. It is time to put on Jesus and forget all this me stuff. Let it go.

It is such a relief when you truly come to the place of realizing that it really is all about Him.

We all say, "It is not about me. It is about Him."

Do you really believe that? If you do, then why are you trying so hard? Why are you trying to make everything happen? Do you not believe that He will make it happen?

Are you trying to make something that you can fall back on? Do you not believe Him?

If you signed on the dotted line, then you can believe Him. No matter how many times you fall, He will still be there to uphold you with His right hand.

DRIVING THE VISION FORWARD

CHAPTER 15 – DRIVING THE VISION FORWARD

> **Habakkuk 2:2** *Then the Lord answered me and said: "Write the vision and make it plain on tablets, that he may run who reads it.*
>
> *3 For the vision is yet for an appointed time; but at the end it will speak, and it will not lie. Though it tarries, wait for it; because it will surely come, it will not tarry.*

I am going to strip the veils in the next couple of chapters between what really makes an apostle versus just a really good leader. There is no doubt that when you look at someone who is in apostolic office, this is someone who is a good leader.

There is so much confusion in the Church today. They say, "I can start a church. Therefore, I am an apostle."

You know, I have seen people start churches that are not even born-again. In some of the State churches (as they are called in Europe), they take the position, because that was the degree that they qualified for. They learned a course on church planting, so they know how to rally the troops and start a church.

There are people like this that say, "Because I can do this, I am an apostle."

No, you are just a really good leader and manager.

So, what makes the difference between somebody who can do the job well and someone who is an apostle?

This is what we are going to be looking at in this chapter. Can we pull back the veil and expose the difference between good leadership and a true apostolic work?

Even for myself, I often questioned my own calling. I said, "Lord, do I even need to be anointed to do some of this stuff?"

You come into contact with so many leaders, even in the world, that have so much talent and skill. If I had to judge them with what many have judged an apostle to be, then I would think that they could be apostles.

So, what defines an apostle and an apostolic work?

If you think I am going to give you all the answers, then you are wrong. You should have questions that you are asking the Lord the answers for. You should be ready to find some answers, not just from me, but also from the Lord yourself.

Each of us walk our own path in fear and trembling and have a conviction of what that calling is. So, let's peel back this question and really get in there.

Dream vs. Vision

I am going to start with this, an apostle is someone who drives the vision forward. How can you have a vision, unless you have first received a vision? Receiving a revelation from the Lord is the first step.

Everyone is saying, "Hold onto your dreams." I even hear Christians saying this.

Do not tell me that what I am doing right now is a dream! I am not completing and holding onto my dreams. What are dreams but a fleshly desire? (James 4:1-3).

Self-made dreams are fleshly desires and cravings, warring within your members that seek to meet your own needs, puff yourself up, and have a nice, happy life with everything you want. That is a dream.

A dream is, "I would like to be happy."

> *The visions that God gives us do not always make*
> *us happy. It often does not make everyone else*
> *happy either. Your apostolic journey does not*
> *start with a dream. It starts with a vision.*

Don't ever tell me to hold onto my dream! I was not born to live out my dream. I was born to complete the call of God on my life, which begins and ends with His vision for my life and for the Church.

Until you have a vision, a revelation from God, then let me tell you something, you are just living out your dreams. That is fine, except for the fact that you are reading a book meant for apostles.

You are not like the rest of the sheep. Forget about your dreams. Die to that flesh already!

So, to clarify - you are not here to fulfill your dreams.

Here is the problem. If all you are chasing after is your dreams, then your dreams and God's vision are going to come into conflict with one another.

Wondering why God has called you to give up home, family, and all these things that you desire? You know why?

He is trying to kill your dreams!

God is not in the business of giving us dreams. He is in the business of giving us mandates, patterns, and visions. Let's really bring a separation. Let's separate the truth from the lie, the light from the darkness. Let's get rid of the pipe dream.

GOD GIVES A DESIRE

Good news though – God, in His grace, gives us a desire to serve Him. Some of us that have submitted to the hand of God and are willing to hear what He wants, our dreams are His visions, and His visions are our dreams, which means we can cling to them.

Yet, I want to smash the worldly thinking. I want to talk about rooting out the spirit of the world in the Church. If you are called to such a ministry, it is not all about reaching your dream one day, where you get everything that you ever wanted.

When you come to the end of your journey, you might find yourself like Paul with your head being chopped off. You could find yourself like Moses being brought to die at the top of a mountain. That is the goal of your dream if you are called to be an apostle.

So, you better be in this for the right reason. Nobody does this for the fun of it.

If all you are doing is chasing dreams, then you are never going to fulfill the vision God has given you.

I am sure that you will accomplish your dream, and I am sure that even God will use it to bless the Church and reach the lost. God is gracious. He will use anything that you give Him. You will have your happy little structure, family, white-picket fence, and happy Christian life.

Others will even come to you and say, "I would like to be a Christian because you guys are all so happy."

You can just go and have that.

I am an apostle, and we do not do happy! We do fire and power!

We do joy, even in the depths of despair. We do peace, long-suffering, kindness, goodness, faith, gentleness, and self-control. That is what we do. We do not do "happy".

STEPS TO ESTABLISHING YOUR MANDATE

Driving the vision forward begins with... receiving a vision. Yet, before that even happens, you and I both know the process of the wilderness and how you had to die to your dreams first. You had to die to the "me, myself, and I".

You had to let go of what you want, what you need, and what your family's desires were. You had to die to that first before God could even begin to give you the vision.

STEP 1: WAITING FOR THE VISION

Returning back to Habakkuk 2:2, see that the vision is received in step 1, which involves waiting for the vision. "Though it tarries, wait for it, because it will surely come."

I am not a patient person. My husband totally gets this passage, but me... not so much.

My husband, Craig, and I fight every time we have to travel. We travel a lot, so you can imagine how much we fight. In my opinion, he takes forever to get ready. You would think that it would be me who takes forever, but it is not.

So, here we are getting ready to leave for another ministry trip. I am trying to be nice because we always fight about the same thing... so I am *trying* not to fight.

I start off nice and gently, "Love, what is the time?"

Rushing past me, "It is a quarter to."

"So, that means we have fifteen minutes, right? Good! I am nearly ready. I will be ready and waiting for you."

Craig: "That is fine."

Me (a little less gently): "Lovey, what is the time now?"

Craig, starting to get "the tone," "We have five minutes."

"Ok, are you nearly ready, love?"

"Yes, love, I am nearly ready."

"Ok, love, I am waiting for you."

I am sitting in the lounge, and it is two minutes passed the time that we are supposed to leave.

"Oh, Lord, help me!"

Of course, behind the scenes, Craig is remembering everything I forgot because I was in such a rush that I did not even bring half the stuff that we need (like the chargers for all our electronic devices...).

The point is that I am not good at waiting. Being the expressive driver that I am, I just want to get in there and get the job done and get it done *now*.

"God, if there is a vision, give me the plan, let me run, let me build, and let me do!" Thank the Lord for His grace and a husband that has the patience to temper me.

I AM IN THE QUIET

Yet, Psalm 1:3 says that when you meditate (take time) on the Lord, you will be like a tree planted by rivers of water. You will bear fruit in every season and have leaves that do not wither, and whatever you do will prosper.

You need time though to sink your roots into the river. We are so busy trying to do the work of God and run the race that we have forgotten to stop and get the vision.

I get so busy. We live in ministry centers. We travel. There is a lot going on. I am preaching, teaching, and writing courses for schools. Then, there is this appointment and that meeting.

Eventually, God had to say to me, "Colette, I am in the quiet."

I said, "Yeah, Lord, I know. I know You are in the quiet."

So, I would go and have my quiet time with Him in the morning as usual. I was sitting there one morning, making sure that He got His hour of the day.

He said, "Colette, you will find me in the quiet."

"Yes, Lord, I know."

"No! No, you don't know. You will find me in the quiet."

"Aha! You want me to go and spend time with You away from the noise?"

You are not the only one that is so stubborn. It took me a while to understand that He meant more than just one little hour in the morning.

You are so busy running, pushing, and striving towards the vision that you do not take time in the quiet. I am not talking about your devotionals. I am not talking about your Bible reading and prayer before you run off to work. I am talking about a season here.

Though it tarries, wait for it. It is about tarrying. However, you are late and have to go to work, so you run out the door. Then, you wonder why you still do not have a vision.

"I'm doing the work," you say.

So, you are a good manager then. Congratulations!

If you want to fulfill an apostolic vision, you are going to have to wait for the vision. You have to give God a chance to speak.

SIGNS: GOD SETS YOU APART – WILDERNESS

You want God to speak on your terms - when you have time, when you are available, and when you have finally finished your career. You will be ready when your kids have finally left home and when your circumstances have shifted.

When it is convenient for you, then you are ready to find your time of quiet. However, it was while Paul was on his way that he was struck to the ground. Before he knew it, he was put three years in the desert - just like that!

Paul was at the height of his career. He had just reached the pinnacle of success. God did not wait until he got his nice severance package from the Pharisee department before He called him. He called him at a rather inconvenient time.

He was at the height of his career. God did not wait for him to retire. God will speak when God wants to speak. However, will we take the time to listen on His terms and not on our terms?

If you have such a call, God is not just going to leave it at that. You have walked in obedience, and you have submitted. Now, if you do not take the time out to listen, He will make you take the time out to listen.

You will find yourself in the wilderness. You will find yourself there because there is nothing, absolutely nothing, in the wilderness. It is just you, the sand, and the odd bird that got lost. That is it.

You think, "Man, I missed God. I missed Him badly. I was striving. I was on my way. I was going to do this great work. Now, it is just me and who even knows what kind of bird that is?"

That's it. There will be nothing. There will be no direction, no prophetic words, no people to minister to.

"I was thriving at the height of my beautiful Pharisee ministry. I thought that was it."

For the season, maybe that was it. Yet, now it is time to get the vision. You will get the vision in the quiet. It will take a little bit more than fifteen minutes before you run out the door. It will be a season.

It is like this because we are very thick-headed. It is not like God is not speaking. We just do not know how to listen half the time. Then, we filter His words through our own desires and dreams.

One wonders how many times God has to separate our dreams from His vision. Even our ministries become a dream instead of a vision.

I dream one day that I can minister to orphans. I dream one day that I can minister to women. I dream one day...

Then, go and start a charity! There are already a lot of people doing that. Those dreams are not an apostolic work. They may be ministries, but we are not talking about a ministry here, are we?

We are talking about an apostolic work! This is why I am making this point so hard.

SOCIAL WORK OR APOSTOLIC WORK?

It is about time we start separating this thinking and maturing the Church. We have billions of social groups and community work. I think that is fantastic, but when are we going to see apostolic works rising up that do more than have a women's ministry and prayer ministry?

We have done this to death. There are a lot of good people covering that ground. Can we please just do what God has given us to do and be willing to pay the price to do it?

One of those first prices is to allow God to separate the vision from the dream. As you are about to learn, just when you catch the vision, the vision grows and evolves. If you do not catch the vision in the first place though, what can God possibly begin to evolve?

> *You cannot evolve a dream. You can just work really hard at it. That does not take the power of God; it just takes the spirit of man who is really determined.*

You can take your own willpower and do it, because many others have done the same thing in times past.

That, however, will not change the Church or the world, will it? We need a little bit more than that. We need a vision.

God will put you in a desperate situation. He will put you in a place like Solomon, where he had to cry out for wisdom. He will put you in a place like Moses, in the middle of the wilderness, where he could only but hear the voice from the burning bush.

You wonder why God is throwing you here and there. Could it be that it is time to get the vision?

You think, feel, and sense, but that is not good enough anymore. If I come up to you and say, "What is your vision?" can you tell me?

I do not mean your vision as in what you *want* to do.

I am saying, "What is the vision that you got from the Father?"

I do not want to hear, "It kind of feels right."

You are not trying on a new pair of shoes here.

"It kind of feels right, but it squeezes a bit by the toes. I think I can wear it in though."

We are talking about a vision from God. It sounds rather odd to say, "It kind of feels right" or "It makes sense because that is what I have always done."

"It seems that this is the way God is leading because that is the anointing that I am flowing in."

Not good enough! What is your vision?

Give me the "Thus saith the Lord" that you got directly from Him!

What did God tell you?

"This is what was prophesied."

Do not get me started on that! Do not base your entire vision on a prophetic word that someone blabbed over you. That is not good enough. What is your vision?

When you were in your wilderness, alone, what was your burning bush experience where you heard the Father say, "My son, my daughter, I am calling you today."

Until you have that, you do not even have a starting point. You do not have the next step in this journey, which is: *Understanding the Vision*.

CHAPTER 16

STEP 2: UNDERSTANDING THE VISION

CHAPTER 16 – STEP 2: UNDERSTANDING THE VISION

I like the part in Habakkuk that says, "and make it plain on tablets".

In the Old Testament, a rather important bit of information was engraved into tablets of stone. Remember what they were?

UNDERSTANDING YOUR VISION: YOUR TEN

COMMANDMENTS

The Ten Commandments. They were written in stone, and they were the core of the Jewish faith.

You are about to discover the difference between vision and mandate.

There is a core "Ten Commandments" revelation that each apostle needs to receive from the Father. You need to have it written on tablets of stone. This is the nucleus of what continues to drive you forward for the rest of your ministry.

Actually, many apostles reading this have already received this from the Lord. However, there is so much other junk smothering it that you have not really held onto those original Ten Commandments. That is why I said in the last chapter that I want to start separating the truth from the lie.

I want to separate what is just good leadership versus apostolic work. I want to separate a dream versus a vision. I want you to put them clearly side by side so that you can make your own decisions of which way you want to go.

You need to receive your core instruction from the Lord. This core instruction you can even receive from a spiritual father or mother. Consider how Solomon received his from David and how Joshua took the Ten Commandments from Moses.

There was a nucleus to the rest of the Law. How each Patriarch walked it out, those commandments were very different. Joshua was a completely different character than Moses. The way that he took the land, and the way that he governed, was completely different to the leadership character of Moses.

Your Core

Yet, the vision was the same, and the core precepts were the same. The Ten Commandments were the same.

"This is the rule, and this is how we will do it."

This is how Craig and I do things in our ministry. We have a unified vision, and we have the "Ten Commandments". I do not want to make this a doctrine, but I just love the difference between the Ten Commandments and the precepts of the law that Moses gave.

I will not go into too much detail on this because I already teach on it in *The Moses Mandate* book. I just want to mention that Moses received two kinds of patterns. He received the Ten Commandments, and he also received all the precepts and the laws.

He got cleaning laws, governing laws, etc. Yet, the Ten Commandments were the nucleus of all of that. If you take all the other precepts, you can link them back to the Ten Commandments.

It is the same in an apostolic work. How you walk out the law and display it is going to be different per person. How Solomon built the temple compared to how David ran the kingdom was completely different.

However, that pattern for the temple remained their Ten Commandments. That remained the same.

How can you go around making rules and laws, and you do not even know why you are doing it? What is the core of your vision?

If I ask you right now to summarize and give me five points that remain in your ministry, regardless of any person that comes in or regardless of their calling, what are the five things that define you as a ministry?

For us, Apostolic Movement International (AMI), those five things are:

1. Training and Equipping
2. Teamwork and Team Building
3. Spiritual Family and Re-parenting
4. Reality – Relationships Without Walls
5. One-on-One Ministry

How we do these things, apostle by apostle and ministry center by ministry center, that changes. Yet, this is the core of who we are as AMI. I am using AMI as an example not to be arrogant, but because you are familiar with this ministry.

So, I want to show you how we do it so that you can pick out what you believe and what your core vision is.

You see, our core is to bring a reality of Jesus to the Church. How we do that though differs from person to person. Yet, at the core, we are a family. We are a team. We are driving forward the reality of Christ in the Church to make her a city set on a hill. That is our core.

> *What is your core? What are your Ten Commandments?*

WHAT HAS REMAINED?

When all that can be shaken is shaken, what remains? What is the one thing that remains steadfast?

When your building is gone, your vision is gone, (or at least what you perceived to be your vision), and everyone has left your ministry – what remains?

Imagine you are standing completely alone before God the Father, and are holding only one stone left in your hand to build with... what is the name of that stone?

That stone is your Ten Commandments.

We get so caught up on the gold of the temple and the rings of the curtains of the tabernacle. We get so hung up on the "do's" and "don'ts" and the "how shall we". We get hung up on "this is how we handle finances", "this is how we take calls", "this is how we minister", or "this is how we do prophetic counseling".

WHEN YOU FORGET YOUR TEN COMMANDMENTS

We get so hung up on all these things that we forget the core. When God is trying to bring you back to the Ten Commandments, He does a little bit of smashing.

> **Hebrews 12:27** *Now this, "Yet once more," indicates the removal of those things that are being shaken, as of things that are made, that the things which cannot be shaken may remain.*

I remember thinking once, this is a fascinating scripture. I should have known better. Just meditate on this scripture for a bit. Focus on that word, "shaken." God was not messing around when He said this.

Those things which "can be shaken" are our dreams, the ideas of man, the ways that we do things, and the rules and regulations that we make. All these things were shaken and removed because they were made by the hands of man.

THE CORE TO REBUILD

Now, the things that cannot be shaken are those that remain. God shakes our ministry often, just to remind us of our Ten Commandments. He reminds us of our core, the nucleus of who we are.

Once you have that, apostle, you can rebuild again and again.

If the tabernacle had been burned to the ground, Moses could have rebuilt it because he had the pattern. If the temple had been taken down, it could be rebuilt again because they had a pattern.

We get so hung up on the work of the ministry that we forget why we are apostles in the first place. We are meant to establish a foundation in the Church.

How are we going to establish a foundation without a pattern? How are you going to establish anything if you have not received the first steps of the blueprint, the core of what you are meant to be doing in the first place?

God will shake you to take you back to your core. The things that can be shaken will be shaken. It kind of makes sense why, firstly, God snatches you away from everything that you have done. Now you understand why He takes away all ministry opportunities and puts you in the wilderness.

Even with the ministry opportunities that you have, you know that you are not really being effective and are not doing what God has put you here to do. Yet, He is not opening up any other doors either.

I will tell you why. You are deaf. You are not listening!

Moses wandered in the desert for a while. Paul had three years in Arabia. How much longer do you want to take? It is up to you.

When are you going to start listening?

"God, I keep trying, but the doors will not open."

Ok, maybe it is the result of spiritual warfare. However, after three years of being in the same condition, I am just going to go with thinking that stupidity is the cause.

You are not stopping long enough to hear the voice of God. He actually does have an open door. He has a ram caught in the thicket right behind you.

Yet, you do not have eyes to see it because you want to see what you want to see. You want to follow the dream that you want to follow and fulfill the ambition that you want to fulfill. Then, you do not understand why the ministry doors do not open.

Why should they open?

You have not even received the vision. Why should you get the Ten Commandments?

SHAKE. SHAKE. SHAKE.

So, God will pull you aside, and then He will start the shaking process. He will shake off what you think ministry is about and what you think you need to do.

You will just start messing up. That is the shaking I am talking about. You will hit the wall and come to the end of yourself.

"I know what mentorship is. I am going to go out and mentor."

Everything falls flat, and you think, "That did not go very well. Everybody left, and I think I messed up a few people along the way. Maybe mentoring is not my thing."

Actually, maybe it is your thing. Maybe you just did not get the nucleus first. Maybe you did not get the Ten Commandments first, and you just went off without the full vision. You thought you could just go out, pick up this new tool, and do the job.

That would be like me going down to the basement, where my husband's tools are, and saying, "This looks handy for something, and this does too. I am going to go and build something."

I would love to see my husband's face if I walked through the house with his circular saw.

"I am just going to go and cut something. I have a picture for something that I want to build. I am just going to use a few of these tools and see how it works out."

I am going to lose digits. There is going to be blood. I suspect that my husband may also lose a few of his power tools.

How foolish! Yet, are we not also doing this with God?

"I know how to preach, prophesy, and mentor a bit. I just went through this great school, so I know how to flow in all the gifts of the spirit and identify ministries. I am just going to go out there and build something."

"Let's see how it goes. Let's go with the flow! Let's wing it with a power drill and a circular saw. Yeah!"

After a little bit of blood, you are going to have a bit of healthy respect for the vision.

> *How many more times do you have to hit the wall before you stop and listen, before you let go of all that stuff and get to the core of what you are meant to be doing? Once you find the core, you will discover the beauty of your real calling.*

STEP 3: DEVELOPING THE PRECEPTS

CHAPTER 17 – STEP 3: DEVELOPING THE PRECEPTS

Now the "how" of walking out those Ten Commandments is found in step three which is about developing the precepts.

This is the trickiest part. It is not tricky because it relies on you to hear the voice of the Lord, but because this is where human error really comes into play. This is where you begin to build the "how-to" of your ministry. This comes through trial and error.

DEFINING YOUR "HOW TO"

Moses came down the mountain with the pattern and the precepts. Then, the daughters of Zelophehad came to the high priest and elders to present their case to Moses. They had no sons in their family and wanted to know what should be done with their inheritance of land. (Numbers 27:1)

Moses had to go back up the mountain again and say, "Lord, what do we do?"

"The daughters of Zelophehad speak what is right; you shall surely give them a possession of inheritance among their father's brothers, and cause the inheritance of their father to pass to them."

Working out the laws was a bit of a trial and error. They had to work it out. Even when it came to dividing the land, Moses had the core, the pattern, but they had to work it out. When they finally got to the Promised Land, some of the tribes found a land that they preferred. They did not want to go over. Moses and Joshua had to make adjustments.

They had to work with God and work the vision out. This is what the scripture calls, "walking out your call in fear and trembling." (Philippians 2:12)

You walk your vision out. You do not get the full picture at the start of your journey.

You have your direction, the core, the Ten Commandments. You know the foundation that you are standing on. Yet, when you begin to build, you put everything up and say, "Actually, I do not like those curtains. That does not work. Let's change that out."

"This room is way too small. If I look at how we have laid this room out, it is not working. We need to make some adjustments here."

You work through the process. This is the third step in driving the vision forward. You need to get the precepts. It takes time. This is the lengthiest part of the process. This is where you make the rules that God had you die to at the beginning so that He could rebuild them correctly. This is where you get the laws.

THE DAY TO DAY BUSINESS

"This is the time we have breakfast at the ministry center. This is the time we have lunch. This is what we serve. This is the time we have dinner. This is who is in charge of all of that."

"These are the resident pastors, and these are the resident apostles of the ministry center."

This is where you find out why you need these things and what the difference between them is (which is a story all of its own).

You might ask us how we came to such a grand revelation of how we run things in our ministry.

It was very simple. What we were doing before was not working. It was blowing up in our face. We were not getting any sleep.

I was crying out, "God, give me something!"

He said two precious words to me… "Resident Pastor."

That means that we do not have to stay up all night, until four o'clock in the morning. Craig and I can just say, "Pastors, deal with that problem".

It sounds so cool. They get to say, "We are the Resident Pastors of the ministry center in South Africa."

I am thinking, "Yeah baby... I passed the buck on God's command. I sure did."

(Kindly do not take every word I pen to mean a doctrinal law for the entire Church. Sometimes, I am just downright ornery and enjoy penning in the reality of what everyone usually thinks but does not often say!)

So the point of that scenario is that we learned the principle of having resident pastors for our ministry centers through trial and error. We kept hitting our heads and getting exhausted. Craig and I kept praying, "Lord, something is not working. What is wrong?"

WORKING IT OUT

At one of our last seminars, I tried to sit down and sum up a bit of what we do. That was a challenge. That is when I realized that I needed to get back to the core Ten Commandments again. We do so much because we live so much.

It is like anything in life. You step out to do something, and it does not work. Why didn't it work? How can we do it differently?

"Lord, give us revelation and wisdom. How do we step out?"

"Ok, that is what we do."

From there, we started building our patterns from how we run our ministry centers to how we handle international travel to how the team operates in a workshop setting versus seminar settings.

We worked out how the team operates for praise and worship, or for when people come for training at one of our centers. We also have a pattern for what is required of those that come.

We did not get all of this in one day, just like Moses did not get the pattern all in one day. Also, David did not build the kingdom of Israel all in one day. In fact, he only started with Judah first before he moved onto the rest of Israel.

David established twenty-four-hour praise and worship. He invented new instruments. The way that we read it sometimes in the Old and the New Testament, it feels like he did it all in one day.

You read of Paul giving Timothy all this instruction on how to run the church. Yet, when you are reading 1st and 2nd Timothy, you are looking at the end of Paul's race. We just read all his epistles as if they happened back to back.

"Wow, Paul came up with all of that in one, big swoop."

No, there were years between the writings of some of those letters. You do not even realize. There were big gaps. He tried, he failed, he learned, he taught. He tried, he failed, he learned, he taught.

If you have been through apostolic training, then you know what I am talking about. You come to the end of yourself. It is called driving the vision forward. There is no shortcut.

This is the time where you cannot throw in the towel and say, "It is never going to work. This is not what I expected."

Of course this is not what you expected. That is why you are an apostle. You are meant to change what is expected. You are not an employee now. You are not a sheep now. You are one that is meant to lead and break ground.

> *You are meant to do something new. You are called to do something that no one else has done. So, why are you surprised that you are experiencing problems that nobody else has had?*

When To Walk Out Your Vision

"Well, since I have the vision, it is all going to go smooth."

Yeah… just like Moses with Korah who had a whole hissy fit at Aaron's appointment. He even had Miriam and Aaron giving him a hard time. Yeah, it was just plain sailing for Moses. He even lost a wife somewhere in the middle of that.

So, it was just plain sailing for Moses, eh?

What about Paul? He had it so easy too, huh? Was it all plain sailing for him because he had a vision?

No, it wasn't plain sailing. He got whipped countless times. He got shipwrecked and almost stoned to death. Then, for the grand finale, he lost his head.

"Oh yeah, I got a vision!"

Good for you. I am glad that you finally waited on the Lord. It only took you thirty years. Fantastic! Praise you, Jesus. You finally got the memo. You got the vision. You now have a starting point.

"I have the core. I have the Ten Commandments."

Awesome. So you know where you are going and why? That is great! You are a lot further ahead than many others, but are you going to walk it out?

"I am just waiting for the right open door."

You know where Paul found his wide open door, right? He found it flat on his face on the pavement. He found his open door when God gave him a back hand.

He did not wait long after that. After just a couple of days, he was standing in the temple declaring the truth.

"When is a good time to start walking?"

When you have the vision and the Ten Commandments, then it is time to begin trial and error. It is like a new creation that you have created, even in the world. They test it and put it through its paces. They tweak this and that until it is perfect, solid, and it works.

YOUR "MAKE OR BREAK" MOMENT

Yet, this is where a lot of people give up. You know why? It is because it is not very glorious. It is so nice to preach and teach, to have lots of speaking engagements, go stand before the crowds, preach and teach, wow them, get in all the finances, and get the fame and fortune.

It is so easy to do that.

What is not easy, however, is getting a knock at your door at three o'clock in the morning and saying, "Jesus, I know that they need Your help, but I really want to hurt them right now."

The price is walking it out, out there in the real world, with real people who are manifesting on you. People who are full of bitterness and junk, who are spewing all of their slime all over you.

At the end of a long ministry day, you do not know what is your demon, their demon, or everyone else's demon. You feel, "Oh Lord, help me."

YOUR MINISTRY EXPRESSION

We have all been there. That is the work of the ministry. That is where you begin to give your ministry personality, expression if you will. You see, you have the core of who you are, but unless I start jumping and shouting, you don't really know what's inside of me, right?

These precepts that God begins to give you are like the expression of your ministry. How many people have you spoken to in the Church and in the world?

They have these grand dreams and visions. They even have the blueprint. They have the picture of how it should run, how it should be laid out, and they have even registered the name of their ministry.

"One day, I am going to do it."

Can I tell you something?

No, you will not!

Today is your "one day". If you already have all of that, "What are you doing? Why aren't you walking it out, apostle?"

"I am waiting for the right circumstance."

As if it was so easy for Jesus to be born in the time that He was and walk out His ministry. He was born in a time of oppression, under the Romans and the Pharisees.

It was not comfortable for Jeremiah and Isaiah either. Even for Daniel, this was not a comfortable time for Israel. In fact, that was the point. They were born at the most uncomfortable times, the most inopportune times, the times when it was not convenient or comfortable for anyone.

So, God chose ones who would be discomforted for everyone! Their names go down in history.

Are you prepared to be discomforted?

It is not just you. It is uncomfortable for everyone. However, who is prepared to pay the price?

"I am just going to sit around and wait."

You will die waiting. Perhaps, if you are lucky, you will fulfill your dream.

Now, I am not saying that it is bad. However, please do not call yourself an apostle. You are a Christian who loves the Lord and has been a tremendous influence to those in the body of Christ and have done your part.

That is fantastic! However, like I said, this is an apostolic book. So, let's get back to the part where we are called to pay the price that nobody else is. God did not give everybody the vision. He gave it to you.

That makes you responsible to go through this stage of figuring it out. Yet, we want it to be easy.

HOW ABOUT JOSHUA?

You know, Joshua got everything from Moses. He got the commandments, and even the precepts, from him. He got the vision from him as well. Moses even laid out the division of the Promised Land. It was a no-brainer.

However, Joshua had to pick up his sword and go take the Promised Land. He had to fight like nobody had ever fought before. He had to give his blood, sweat, and tears, in his seventies and eighties.

He had to call up Caleb, and the two of them led God's people to take the land. Joshua had to challenge them long after Moses was gone. He had the anointing, the power, everything. Yet, he still had to walk it out for himself.

He still had to face the trial and error. He had to face the battles and find out what worked and what did not.

Remember that big mess up that he made with the city of Ai? (Joshua 7) He had to learn for himself.

If he would have quit before they even hit Jericho, all the planning and precepts would not have been received.

He got it all. He got his pattern. However, if he had not taken the land, walked it out, and messed up a little, then he would not have driven the vision forward.

So, there is no place to worry about messing up. Here is something that is going to help you out with that:

> *You do not have to mess up a little. You have to mess up a lot! You are an apostle.*

There is a scripture where Paul says, "Consider your calling, brethren, not many wise were called, but rather the foolish."

If that word is for believers and leaders, in general, how much more does that apply to the apostle? We are at the top of the "foolishness parade". We have messed up more than anyone else.

SIGNS: HITTING ROADBLOCKS. MAKING SOLUTIONS

Let me tell you. I have messed up more than most. That is why I am able to stand and do what I do. You see, it was never about me. All things work together for good for those who love the Lord and are called according to His purpose.

If you are afraid to mess up, you will never step forward. If you step forward without the commandments and the vision, don't even try to make precepts.

I love this part about precepts. For some of us, doing the precepts is hard. We just want to go and have the picture already done. We just want to have all the fun stuff. Having to go through trial and error, failing and succeeding, is not fun.

Then, you have those that have an opinion for everything.

"If I was going to go and make a law, I think I would make it like this."

Where is your vision exactly? Where are your Ten Commandments, and what qualifies you to make those precepts? Go through the process.

I am sure, even as you are reading, that you see in your own life, and see in others, to just take one and not the other. They just have the vision, but they are not prepared to pay the price.

They may also have the Ten Commandments, but they are not prepared to go through the trial and error. On the other hand, they are prepared to go through the trial and error and work it out, but they do not know where they are going.

They just go here, there, and everywhere, trying to see what works, but nothing works.

No, there is a very specific order. Tarry. Wait on the Lord, and let Him write on your heart, so that you can fulfill your purpose.

> **Leviticus 26:3** *If you walk in My statutes and keep My commandments,* **and perform them…**

I am a big advocate of obedience. We think that obedience is it, but there is a bit more than that. You have to walk in the Spirit. You have to be obedient and keep the commandments, but then you have to perform them…

This is a very big "doing word". "Perform" means to walk it out. It is not good enough to get the commandments or the statutes and the law. You have to walk it out. I love this next part.

> *4 Then I will give you rain in its season, the land shall yield its produce, and the trees of the field shall yield their fruit.*
>
> *5 Your threshing shall last till the time of vintage, and the vintage shall last till the time of sowing; you shall eat your bread to the full, and dwell in your land safely.*

We were talking about dreams and visions in the previous chapters, but see here how God works from visions to dreams. When you do it His way, He will take care of you. Yet, even if He does not, that is not the point. You walk out His commandments and be obedient.

He will take care of the details. You will face the test so that you can make the right rules. Your steps are ordered by Him. Every time you have a stumbling block, you go to Him and get wisdom. He will give it, and it will be like building blocks to your vision.

How do you know if you are in this place?

When I spoke about the wilderness, I made it very easy to see whether you are there or not - God just takes you out completely. He takes you out so that you can get the Ten Commandments. He shakes and shows you what's wrong.

"That's wrong, that's deception, that's demonic, you should not have picked that up... where did you even find that from? It must go!"

He starts taking things out. However, you know you are in the stage of getting the precepts when you are having a lot of problems that you have to solve every single day.

PROBLEMS ARE KNOCKING...

You wake up, and a problem knocks on the door. You check your email, and a problem jumps out at you.

Do you know why God is giving you problems? It is not to get you down. It is so that you might solve them. It is so that you can create an expression for your ministry. Then, no matter what the devil throws at you, or the world throws at you, you have an answer for that.

In our ministry, it is like... I have a book for that.

People ask me how and why I write so many books. This is why – problems, people! I had rebellious team members with bigger problems than me. People were attacking me, we had financial difficulties, and there was one road block after another.

I said, "Lord, help!"

Eventually after repeating myself one hundred times, I said, "I am going to write this down. The next one that has such a manifestation, I am going to give them the book. They can read the book, and then we can lay hands afterwards. I am tired of repeating myself."

That is why I have a library, and it is growing daily. I write them because we need them. I need them to train my team, and those God sends us, to reach the world. It just so happens that writing the books also blesses the body of Christ. That is the character of our ministry.

God uses what He needs to use, so that you can grow and get an expression. You look at all these problems and say, "It is not fair. Why am I having all these problems that nobody else is having?"

Why are you complaining? You will have solutions that nobody else has either!

Think about the one thing that defines you, the answers that you do have. Why do you have that answer, and please tell me why you are so convinced of them?

It is because you had to bear long. You and I both know that you went through. There is no demon in hell that will ever take that from you. That principle was birthed in the fire because you did not just hit a road block - you hit the very fires of hell. You had to claw your way up with your bare hands, and that is why you stand where you do today.

You are a trailblazer. You are meant to go ahead and not just "prepare the way."

It sounds so good when you say that you are going to "prepare the way." However, you are meant to go through. That is how you are going to prepare the way.

You are going to go through before everybody else goes through. When you are at this point where you have gone through, hitting road block after road block and getting solution after solution, then you are finally ready to put your team together.

STEP 4:
APOSTOLIC TEAMS

CHAPTER 18 – STEP 4: APOSTOLIC TEAMS

You will get to this point of saturation where you have the vision, you have the Ten Commandments, you have the precepts and rules, but then you start running out of daylight hours and discover, "Aha, I am not a one-man army."

My husband reminds me of this, every single day, but yet I still forget.

"You are not a one-man army, Colette. You have a team. Why don't you let them help you?"

You get to a point where you have done all that you can in yourself. You have gotten the vision, you have birthed this baby, you have gone through, and then you reach a point where you are on a plateau.

I would like to say that it is more like you reach a glass ceiling. You can see where you need to go, and you feel where God is taking you. You know that you have walked in obedience, you have walked in the statutes, He has opened the doors, and you are doing what you can.

Yet, the growth is just not going anywhere. You need a team. It is time, as Moses did, to bring on the seventy elders.

THE TEAM

What was Moses doing? Moses sat there from first thing in the morning till last thing at night. I understand Moses. Everybody was coming to him with all of their little itty bitty problems.

"Should we put this in the dishwasher or not, Moses?"

"No, that does not go in the dishwasher. We wash those by hand because I spent $200 on that knife. If you trash it, I am going to be very upset (to put it mildly)."

"Ok, next question."

"Should we paint it this color or that color?"

"Should we park here or there?"

"Should I minister here or there?"

"I have a prophetic word. Should I share it now or later?"

I feel Moses sitting and judging every single day. He was sitting there from morning to night, answering every question and handling every problem and crisis.

Then, Jethro came along and said, "Moses, come on. You are killing yourself. Something has to change. Moses, you need a team. You have the vision, the commandments, the statutes, but you really need a team to distribute the load."

Thank the Lord that Moses did what he did because even when you look at Ezra and Nehemiah when they dedicated the temple, you will notice that, even though Ezra stood up and declared the word, they had all the scribes and priests go amongst the people and express the word and teach them one on one. (Nehemiah 8)

He could not do it one on one. They were a massive people - a multitude. He needed help. At this point, a lot of people hit a plateau, and they stay there. They stay there because they build a ministry that is revolved around themselves.

The problem is that you can only do so much as one person. You know what will happen? You will go back to the pulpit hopping thing because it is a lot easier.

We were joking because we have done a lot of ministry tours over the last few years. I said, "If I did not have to host the seminar, lead the worship, do the prophesying and everything else, but just had to get up and preach, I could do it every single day without a problem."

That is the easy part. The Holy Spirit comes. He picks me up, He pours me out, and I get it again the next morning. If I can spend time with the Lord, eat, not make any decisions or plans and just get up and preach, I can do it with my eyes closed.

However, all the other stuff is dramatic. It is hard work. There is bickering and fighting, who is in charge of this and who is going to host that?

Those kind of details are what is exhausting.

POINT OF SATURATION

So, what happens, as a leader, is that you get to this point of potential where you finally start rising up and have all these ambitions, plans, and hopes, but you can only do so much. You have a decision to make, but you look around and either do not trust anyone, or you do not get the concept that you need a team and not just servants.

So, you end up just doing the "pulpit thing". That is great. You are reaching the masses and preaching to the same kind of multitude that crucified Jesus. It is great that they heard the gospel. That was a massive part of His mandate, but it was the twelve Disciples who changed the Church.

Today, we stand on the foundation of the Disciples and of Paul, whom Jesus invested into, again and again. Paul stood in front of crowds too, but it was his investment into his spiritual sons that counted.

When you read his Epistles, you get this man. Read his teachings, and you know without a doubt that he was the real deal. You see clearly the daily work he did with his team that caused him to change the face of this world.

He spearheaded a movement. We are talking about an apostolic movement here. It is going to take more than one person to start this movement.

It is going to take people who are in sync with the same vision, pushing and driving this vision forward. You cannot maintain this on your own. You have to start running with the vision. You have to put the team together.

PUTTING THE TEAM TOGETHER

This is how you know that you have reached this point of readiness. Firstly, you become saturated with your load. You have done everything that you can, preached everything that you can, and you start hitting a glass ceiling.

You are a human, and you can only do so much in one day. God did not call me at a convenient time either. He called me when I had two small children, aged one and two.

It was not a convenient time to suddenly go into the ministry. That He even provided for us to travel was miraculous. We came from South Africa. We were broke and living with family. Craig did not even have a job at the time.

It was miraculous how God pulled us out. Then He sent us to Mexico of all places. Fast forward a few more years, and I had another child on my hip. All three of my daughters were unplanned pregnancies.

When I say that God puts pressure, I am not messing around.

IT'S INCONVENIENT. EMBRACE THIS REALITY

So, I now have these three kids. By then, we had started our first prophetic school. I had started that already before I even fell pregnant with Rebekah. It was not convenient. I was breastfeeding as I started writing some of the teachings for *Practical Prophetic Ministry*.

It was not convenient. I learned to grow through those pressures, through trial and error. Then came stage four where God started to expand us.

You can only do so much, and then you are finished with your own resources. God was so good though. We took over the work from my father, so I already knew the concept of teams. We stepped into the next transition already equipped with a team.

Regardless of that, I was still trying to do it all by myself. I trusted myself to do the job properly. I said to myself, "I am the only one that remembers anyway. I am the only one that has the 'Ten Commandments'. I am the only one who has the vision."

Of course, I was the only one that God could talk to… right?

I was so boastful about my vision that I forgot who it came from. Then, I got a nice, strong smack, a strong word of correction from my spiritual son one day.

Nathan looked at me and said, "Mom, it is time to let go. It is time that you start trusting us to do this job. You are killing yourself. Stop it!"

He was right. And from there, the process began. I started to give out the responsibility and care so that they could fail, instead of me, for a change. That was so nice. Had I known what a pressure it would have taken off me, I would have done it years before.

However, I was carrying it, I was going through the death, I was doing the trial and error, making the mistakes, going through blockage after blockage, breakthrough to breakthrough… no wonder why I was tired.

The crazy thing was that the minute that they picked up the load, they started going back to the steps I had been walking. God started pulling them away to get the vision, to be reminded of the core principles, and to start building up the precepts.

Each one of them started failing and messing up. At first I was like, "Lord, what have I done? Have I just destroyed the entire ministry in one swoop, just like that?"

So often, I just wanted to jump in and save the day.

"Guys, be careful! You need to…" I had to bite my tongue, saying, "Shut up, Colette, shut up Colette."

That takes more courage than anything else in the world. Letting go is so much harder than picking up. I did not know that until I went through the process. Putting your trust in others and passing the law, precepts, and vision out until it becomes theirs is what you must do.

Only then can they run with you and accomplish the vision.

SIGNS: IMPLEMENTATION

The Lord will start opening the doors if you do not have a team. He will start opening the doors for you to start sharing that load with others. I said something on Facebook once.

The apostle has a team that builds with him, not for him.

When I say the word "team", I am not talking about someone that can just serve the coffee and tea.

Yeah, we learned some precepts along the way on how someone should be trained up to become a team member. However, that is not what I mean by "team". I mean someone that can take the vision and drive it forward with you - part of an apostolic team.

If you are going through this process for the first time and are ready for a team, then God will start bringing you team members.

If God is not bringing you team members, it is because you are not ready for a team.

Did you go through the other steps yet? Did you wait on Him? What are your Ten Commandments and your precepts? In the trial and error stage, where are you? Are you ready for a team to pass that onto?

You need to be saturated and at a point of your limit where you cannot do anymore. Was all of what you went through led by the Holy Spirit? If that was led by the Holy Spirit, then the door will open by the leading of the Holy Spirit as well.

I love the part in Habakkuk where it says "that he may run who reads it." You have to write down the principles so that he may run who reads it. He cannot run if he has not read it. He cannot read it if it has not been written.

People just want teams. So many people come to our ministry and say, "Wow, I wish I had a team like yours."

I am thinking... "You have no idea what it is like to have a team. You want them? Let's see if you can live with them for one day. They will run circles around you."

This is because they are not just my lackeys who do the work. They stand next to me, shoulder to shoulder. They did not just come premade, like from Ikea. They don't just come in a box, you put the pieces together, and then have yourself a rocking chair.

"You are so lucky to have a team."

Let me just stop you right there. You have no idea. These are ones whom God gave. We went through the process together. This is their vision as much as mine.

Not many people are willing to pay that price. For those of you who are willing to pay that price, this is why you have had to pay that price. This is why God has taken you the long way round.

If He has taken you through that, then He will bring you those team members. However, for those of you who already have teams, you will reach a point where your team has to go to the next level.

They need to come and stand shoulder to shoulder. This means that it is time for you to back off and put that load of responsibility on them, so that you can start the process all over again.

STEP 5: DRIVING THE VISION FORWARD

CHAPTER 19 – STEP 5: DRIVING THE VISION FORWARD

The last stage is driving the vision forward. Actually, the last four points that I have been talking about have just been about establishing the vision. Now, you have your vision, your Ten Commandments, your precepts, and you have put your team together.

You are running this race, and you have laid aside every weight and sin that so easily besets you. Yet, this is still not enough.

> *You need to realize that structure maintains, but a vision imparts power.*

STRUCTURE IS NOT ENOUGH

As you have gone through the precepts, you have established a structure without realizing it. When someone says, "How do you do that in your ministry?" you should be able to tell them. That was in phase three.

They should be able to ask you any questions. "How do you deal with demons in your ministry?"

"How do you usually run conferences?"

"How do you train someone?"

We have precepts for all these things. We have a structure. However, it takes more than a structure to drive a vision forward. You need power. The people will perish without a vision.

Up until now, if you were a really good leader, you could probably do a lot of those points. You could push through with your strengths, you could have a dream, and you could push through. Yet, now you are at a point where you have your structure and your ministry, but how do you take it to the next level?

This is where you begin the process over again, because your vision must evolve. This is the point that so many misunderstand. Then, God has to take drastic measures to take them back through the shaking again.

You received your vision how many years ago?

I do not know about you, ladies and gentlemen, but I certainly do not look the same today as I did twenty years ago. Let's be kind to one another, shall we? Certain things had to evolve like my clothing size and hair style.

Certain things had to change. I could not stick to the old way that I used to dress. I cannot do things the same way today as I did things when I was single or newlywed. I had to evolve as a person. As I matured, as people around me changed, as we traveled and came into contact with many different people, I had to evolve.

AVOIDING DEATH OF A VISION

This is something that is so difficult. If you do not get this, you will experience death of a vision after death of a vision. You will not understand why. However, there is a shortcut.

If you have been through death of a vision, I am telling you right now that there is an easier way. You can evolve the vision. You can take it from one form to another. Otherwise, you will hit a plateau.

I spoke before about hitting a glass ceiling. You are so full of potential and want to reach further, but you need a team so that you can. Even after that, if you do not allow your vision to evolve, you will eventually hit a plateau.

LETTING THE VISION EVOLVE

It will be a very well organized plateau, a very successful plateau, but still a plateau nonetheless. We see this in many traditional denominations and churches.

There are these great moves of God. They have the vision, they have their doctrine, they have their precepts, they know how they are going to ordain their ministers, and they have all their laws and bylaws beautifully established. There is fantastic organization. They even have teams of pastors, ministers, and leaders that are set in place.

They have their hierarchy, and it was, in that time, glorious. Yet, today, let's take a look at the Methodists, the Baptists, and many other denominations. They all started out with fire, but where are they today?

They are flat-lining. Why is this? It is because the vision needed to evolve.

"No, no, no. That is the vision we got many years ago. We are keeping it this way."

Imagine the reign of David for a moment. The children of Israel took the Promised Land many years before. With the help of David, they built on the Promised Land. In his time, they were finally eating the grapes and figs that God promised.

Then the grand finale. David brings back the ark. Did he go to all that effort to just put it into another tent? No, he set about making a plan to put it into a temple.

Why build a tent when you own the land?

When they were in the wilderness, they needed a tent. They were traveling from place to place, so they really did need something easy to transport. Yet, now the land had been established.

They had the City of David.

Here David gets an entirely new pattern, but not so new that it threw Moses out.

I would say that the pattern he got was "new and improved" – an evolution of the original. We see this right through the Scriptures. Remember that even Ezra built a new tabernacle?

Again, it was a new and improved pattern. It was a little different. It was not as glorious as Solomon's because they did not have gold to splash around, but it worked for that time and season.

COMPREHENDING TIMES AND SEASONS

You see, the core remained the same, but how they put it together evolved. The vision was added to, taken away from, and adapted for that time and season. If you are reading this, then you understand the concept of times and seasons.

There are many seasons in your life that God takes you through. This process that I am talking about is not a once-off thing. Here is something that you need to realize:

You are going back to the beginning again.

Step five is step one.

"I got my vision. I spent years establishing it. We are organized and sorted out."

Next thing you know, the Lord is saying to me again, "Colette, you will find me in the quiet."

Here we go again…

That which can be shaken is usually shaken. God started to shake this beautiful, well-established structure all over again from the beginning.

You say, "Why, Lord?"

He says, "Because you asked for more. What did you think was going to happen? It is time for the vision to evolve."

However, you are still stuck on the vision from twenty years ago. You are still trying to flog a dead horse. Let the horse die! It died back then for a reason, and it will die again.

You are not the person that you were back then, your circumstances are not what they were back then, and the people around you are not what they were back then. The core part of your vision will always be the same.

For example, for our ministry, Apostolic Movement International, being made up of trainers, leaders, and family has always been the same. However, becoming spiritual parents was an entire shift of the vision. That evolved things completely.

Up until then, I was just a mentor, and I wanted to equip the body of Christ.

In order to do that though, the Lord said, "You need to add this aspect to your vision."

God pulled us aside. He had Craig and I fight and work on our marriage for a couple of years. He pulled us to the backside of the desert so that we could fight with one another. We did that until we sorted it out.

I was like, "Lord, what is going on?"

"There is coming a time when your marriage, your family, and your life is going to be a glass house. You sort this out now! I need this relationship, and this family, to be a vessel for my use."

We went right back to the beginning, and the shaking began. All the bad things in our marriage, the experiences we had, and the rules we made were addressed.

He started making us into a team. The vision had to evolve. As we changed, the vision changed too. From that time, God started to bring us more and more spiritual children because we were finally ready to have them.

Every time your vision and your ministry reaches a plateau, God will shake it up and say, "It is time to evolve."

Yet, you can be so stubborn and sit on that plateau for years. You can taste it. You know that there should be more, and you want God to just add "the more" to you. However, it is a process. Think about the process that you went through at the beginning. You have to go through this process again.

If you stop being so stubborn and take the time to listen, to revisit your Ten Commandments, then you will see if God has something that He wants to add to you.

Spiritual parenting was not on the memo when we first started out. Training was all that there was going to be. Praise and worship was not part of it. There was so much that was not part of the original core that we started with.

It was all just training, and that was it. That was our nucleus. We just wanted to see the Church as a city on a hill and train God's warriors. That was it. I did not even know how we were going to do that.

Then, God added the fivefold ministry, spiritual parenting, and prophetic praise and worship. He started evolving us as a ministry, and still today, we continue to grow.

Manager vs. Apostle

I mentioned at the beginning how I want to separate the difference between manager and apostle. I have written down some points here because I want you to realize that they are not the same thing.

Up until now, perhaps you have been "taking care of business".

God wants you to do more than just take care of business. He wants you to begin building. He wants you to evolve and catch the vision.

He wants you to put together the structure for that vision. He wants you to bring your team together. Where are you at today?

If you have not started, then you now have the cheat sheet. Look again through the points and see which one you are at.

Below, I have listed some of the differences between manager and apostle:

MANAGER: POLICES THE RULES

APOSTLE: ESTABLISHES THE RULES

A manager is one who polices the rules. You know all those precepts we spoke about? A manager is one who takes care of those details. We love managers, and we need them. In our ministry, we have a bunch of them.

I thank God for it, but make no mistake, this is someone you can hire to do this job. They just need to take care of business. They make sure everyone starts answering the phones at 9am and clocks off work at 5pm.

They make sure that the correspondence is handled correctly. This is vital, and I love these guys. For many, it is their ministry. I am not saying that it is not a ministry. I am just saying that it does not define an apostle. We confuse these two sometimes.

An apostle is one who establishes the rules. He is the one who makes them (through the inspiration of the Word and Spirit). No surprise there. He is the one who went through the process.

MANAGER: TAKES CARE OF THE DETAILS

APOSTLE: THINKS OF DETAILS EVERYONE ELSE MISSED

A manager takes care of the details.

An apostle walks in and says, "You missed, this, this, and this. This does not line up with the precepts."

The apostle comes with the plumb line and catches all the details that you missed. A manager can take care. He has his checklist to sort things out. An apostle does not need the checklist. He is the checklist because he is the ministry.

He does not need to remember everything. You do not always have to remind them of everything. For me, you just need to remind me of what to pack. Thank the Lord for my husband who always helps me with that!

When it comes to the work of the ministry, people say, "How do you remember all these things?"

I say, "I don't. I just am."

We did not make up these things by remembering. We had to eventually vocalize our rules, but most importantly, we are the rule.

You, as an apostle, have been through the process. That is why the apostle remembers. He picks out the details, because he walks in and goes, "That does not feel right. Why does this not feel right? What is missing?"

It is like putting on shoes that are too tight or a jacket that does not fit. Something is not working.

MANAGER: CONCERNED ABOUT THE JOB AT HAND

APOSTLE: CONCERNED ABOUT THE CONDITION OF EVERYONE'S SPIRIT

A manager concentrates on the job at hand. A manager will walk into a meeting and say, "We do not have enough water bottles. The sound is not working. Do we have enough chairs for everybody?"

I love managers. They make my life very easy. However, an apostle walks in and says, "Ok, who is walking in the flesh? I felt you all the way upstairs in my hotel room. I will not stand here and preach with that oppression. Who is going through?"

This is someone who has gone through the fire a bit. They can notice the details, but the first thing that they will feel and be worried about is the condition of the work and the team. They are not just playing house. They are not afraid to get in and get involved in people's lives.

MANAGER: WORKS WITH HIS EYES SET ON THE TASK

APOSTLE: WORKS WITH HIS EYES SET TOWARD THE FUTURE

The manager works with his eyes on the task. He says, "We have this, this, and this to do. Guys, we have a lot of ground to cover today. You will handle attendees... you will lead the prophets in prayer... and you will check the sound equipment."

We need these managers, but the apostle is not one who is looking down. He is one who is looking forward. He is assuming that all of that is already taken care of. He knows that once those jobs are done, it is time to start the itinerary for the next year already.

"God tells me that we are starting an apostolic move, which means that we have to go to the States, South Africa, and Germany. We need to start praying in those mighty warriors now!"

That is the difference. If God has called you to be an apostle, what are you doing? It is good that you can be a manager and that you can take care of the details. In fact, that is part of your training, but it takes someone with the vision to drive it forward.

MANAGER: GETS WISDOM FOR TODAY

APOSTLE: ALREADY HAS THE VISION AND PLAN FOR TOMORROW

A manager gets wisdom for today. In fact, a lot of the precepts, the managers helped me to work out. They would come to me and say, "We hit this snag today. How do we work it out?"

So I go before the Lord, I get revelation, and we sort out the problem. However, the apostle is already way beyond that. He is not looking at the problems today. He is looking at the problems tomorrow.

He already has the vision and the plan for tomorrow. He already knows the problems we will be facing later and what God has already told him.

MANAGER: GOOD AT MAINTAINING A WORK

APOSTLE: GOOD AT BIRTHING A WORK

A manager is good at maintaining a work. They are the ones, once you bring your team together and have your precepts, who will make sure it is maintained. It can also be an apostolic function, but it does not define an apostle in office.

You can maintain the work, pay the bills, and make sure all the rules are done. You can make sure that the team is taken care of and that the pastors are doing their jobs. You can go around and take care of business, but it takes an apostle to birth a work and not just maintain it.

It takes an apostle to drive the vision forward, to evolve that vision again and again. Yes, we need someone who can take care of the details. We need someone who has managerial skills to help pull it together.

However, that does not define an apostle. That takes a manager. If you want to be an apostle, it is going to take a lot more than just doing the job.

MANAGER: CONSIDERS WHAT HE DOES WORK

APOSTLE: CONSIDERS WHAT HE DOES MINISTRY

A manager considers what he does work. He is exhausted at the end of the day because of all the work that he had to do and the fires that he had to put out.

An apostle goes to bed at night and says, "Today, I did the ministry." He does not consider anything that he does work. He considers it ministry, whether what he did was administration or to stand behind the pulpit.

I do not consider what I do every day a job. I do not consider it a career, and I do not consider it work. I do not like saying that I have worked hard. If I ever complain, I am saying, "I have poured out so much that I feel like a dead rag. I need to go before the Lord again. I need to get filled up."

Whether I am writing an email or handling a problem at the bank, I am doing the work of the ministry, not just business as usual. I know that I am playing with words, but if you are always just thinking like a manager, then you are never going to drive the vision forward.

VISION EVOLUTION

If it is all about the work, the structure, the doing, and the maintaining, then you are never going to drive the new vision forward. You are never going to adapt what God has already given to you.

We are going to look a bit at how apostles can work together, how leaders can work together. Every single one should be driving the vision forward.

When you have a group of apostles that all share the same vision, you drive it forward together, and it is very possible. This is true, especially if you have your Ten Commandments. Each one as they walk it out will walk it out their way.

The way they express the law and the structure and put it together will shift and change, according to each one. However, you have your core - your nucleus. This means that you are in a position to reproduce yourself.

When you are at a place where you can drive a vision forward, you have done all five of these points, you have taken your time with God, gotten the commandments, precepts, put your team together, and evolved that ministry to the next level, then, and only then, are you ready to impart that vision to others and duplicate it into them so that they can take it further as well.

5 STEPS TO ESTABLISHING YOUR MANDATE

1. Vision
    - The birth of your mandate
2. Commandments
    - The core principles that define you
3. Precepts
    - The pattern to which you build (blueprint)
4. Implementation
    - Building the pattern you have
5. Driving the Vision Forward
    - Changing with the seasons – adding to the vision

THE APOSTOLIC FUNCTION

CHAPTER 20 – THE APOSTOLIC FUNCTION

When I was young and first got on fire for the Lord and wanted to do the work of the ministry, I wanted everything to happen tomorrow. I had to do everything today because the world was going to change tomorrow.

Do you remember those days?

Then, the Lord tempers you a bit, and you realize that you do not just need a daily plan, but a yearly plan. You realize that the Lord moves in times and seasons. All we need to do is remain obedient.

As you take those steps in His time and season, you will see the doors open, see the land shift, and see Him do what you cannot do.

Again, I want to remind you that it is your part to be obedient, but it is His part to make you into the vessel you need to be.

You cannot shape yourself. You cannot make yourself into an apostle or prophet.

You cannot call yourself or empower yourself. This is a calling from the most high God. He who has called you will complete His work in you. He will equip. He will shape. He will bring you to the cross.

S.O.S. SUBMIT. OBEY. SERVE.

You cannot even crucify yourself. All you can do is recognize the nails and give up the ghost. Your place is to submit, obey, and serve. When you do these things for the Lord, He equips, empowers, and releases you to do the things that you need to do.

I want to bring you to rest. You are trying so hard to do the work of God, to find your call, to get the answers, to be the apostle, prophet, teacher, evangelist, or pastor. Whatever it is, you are trying so hard.

You started in grace. Now are you going to end in works? Did you forget why you are on this road?

The greatest challenge that I have for you is S.O.S.
The rest is up to the Holy Spirit, and we forget that
sometimes.

You get so busy training your mighty men, identifying them, and applying all the principles. You get so hung up on the principles that you forget why you are here. At the end of the day, when all the principles are gone, all your strength is gone, and you have nothing left, that is when you realize that it is the hand of God that put you here.

It is the hand of God that will keep you here. You have to trust Him to do what you cannot do. You have to trust Him in spite of your sin and your failure. In spite of pushing through, in spite of what people say, in spite of the teams that let you down, and in spite of the mistakes you have made, you have to trust God more than you trust yourself.

You have to trust Him more than you trust your weakness and more than you trust others to let you down. You must trust God more.

This is not about the title or the position. This is about doing what you were put on this earth to do. Although I am speaking about the apostle, I hope, at the same time, I am tearing away the title "Apostle", because it is not about the position, but about the work that God has called you to do.

It is time for you to put your hand to the plow. It is time to count the costs. It is time to look at the building materials and see how much it will cost you to build this magnificent temple, this city on a hill, that God has called us all to build.

It is time to stop playing around with what "I" want and what "I" feel. It is not about "my" ministry or what "I" think. It is time that you start doing, building, and establishing God's will in the earth.

If I have to do the work of God as somebody who has no title, just a little pawn on the chessboard, then I will be that pawn on the chessboard. I do not have to be a bishop, a knight, or the queen.

As long as I am in the hand of God, and in His will, there is nowhere else where I would rather be. I would rather be a doorkeeper in the house of the Lord, a nothing, and know that I am in His will than boast in my ministry titles.

Knowing that I am the most anointed doorkeeper that there is, empowered to keep that door is enough rather than a king upon his throne, ruling in my own pride and not His will.

Every single one of us has a part to play. We have a position ordained by God, not man. Yes, as leaders, God needs us to help others recognize that ordination in their lives. That is certainly a big part of what the apostle does.

Yet, as we look at the apostolic function in this chapter, I want to lay the weight of the Church on your shoulders, apostles. I want you to feel the responsibility of the title. I want you to bear the care of the Church upon yourself.

I want you to feel the intensity of what we are called to do. It is no longer about what your calling is, what your vision is, what your place is. But whatever your hands can find to do today, may you indeed do it with every breath that is in you.

Let us run this race that is set before us and lay aside every weight and sin that so easily besets us, so that we might run with endurance.

Every one of us has a different race to run. Every one of us looks ahead with a task at hand. You are never going to complete the task at hand tomorrow if you do not deal with the task at hand today.

If all you are aiming for is reaching your mandate and vision "one day", doing that one great thing one day, then you will miss what God has called you to do today.

Can I bring you to contentment, to peace? What if all God needs you to do is sit at His feet and worship Him? What if that is all that God requires of you? What if you have gone through all the death, suffering, and rejection to do nothing but tell Him, "I love you", because you were born as a vessel to worship Him?

BACK TO SIMPLICITY

Adam and Eve fellowshipped with the Father in the Garden of Eden. Do you know what their calling was? It was to fellowship with God and take care of the garden. So simple.

Our first ministry is to the Father, and we so easily forget that. Yes, we are going to look at a bunch of fantastic, juicy principles and get your mind ticking, and your spirit soaring. I am going to remind you why you are here.

Yet, before I go there, might I just bring you back to the child in you that was called so long ago, in your foolishness, your weakness, and selfish ambition. God saw through all of that and determined that you would be called a mighty warrior, a king or queen of the most high God.

Can we please go back to why we stand here today?

Before we put all the stripes on our shoulders, and the badges across our chest, and wear all our medallions to prove to the world why we are so magnificent, can we go back to the seed of the apostleship within us?

We have a heart that beats for something new. We are willing to pay the price to change, not just the Church, but our communities and nations. Feel the weight of that and remember that you are never going to be able to carry all that weight with your talent, skill, and principles.

God did not call the big, strong gladiator. He called the shepherd boy with nothing but a sling and a stone to take down Goliath.

So, as we look at the apostolic function, how do you know when you are doing your job?

DEFINING: APOSTLE. APOSTOLIC. APOSTLESHIP.

When it comes to the ministry of the apostle, some people say, "I am an apostle" and others say, "I am apostolic." Then, you have those that say, "I am doing an apostolic work."

In all of that, we are all trying to figure out what an apostle is supposed to do. We want to know, "As an apostle, how do I know if I have done my job?"

That is the crux of what we are going to look at in the rest of the book. How can you begin to tell me if you have done your job if you do not know what your job is?

It is like that in the workplace. How can your boss come and say, "You have done a fantastic job," if you do not have a job description?

What are you called to do?

So, we are going to look at two aspects, your mandate and your purpose, in fulfilling that mandate. We will also look at how you will know if you are on track.

Looking even broader, how do you know when an apostle has done the work that he is meant to be doing in the Church? How do you identify not just the character of the apostle?

I have spoken to you about the character already. I have given you a picture of what an apostle looks like in *The Apostolic Handbook*. I want to go a little deeper now. I want to talk about what he is supposed to be doing, what his function is.

When all is said and done, can you tick off the list that says "I have done my job?"

Will the Lord be able to say, "Good and faithful servant, you have completed what I have given you to do?"

Like in all other things, we need to start at the beginning. We need to ask ourselves what our job is in the first place, to know whether or not we have fulfilled its requirements.

DEFINING THE MANDATE

I am going to talk about six apostolic mandates. As I share on each one of these from the Word, you are going to see the different places that God has taken you. If you are an apostle, or feel that you may be one, perhaps you can already begin to identify some of these patterns in your life.

Dictionary Definition for Mandate:

Any contract by which a person undertakes to perform services for another.

Strong's Concordance – Apostle:

652 apostolos {ap-os'-tol-os}

AV - apostle 78, messenger 2, he that is sent 1; 81

1) a delegate, messenger, one sent forth with orders

1a) specifically applied to the twelve apostles of Christ

Pattern, commission... these are words that we can look up in the Word. The purpose of why you have been put on this earth. An apostle has a mandate. A prophet has a mandate. You have an end goal - the thing that you were born to do.

I am going to look at these six different types specifically, and there are some things that I want you to recognize. Think for yourself as I go through each of these. I am not going to give you all the answers - you are an apostle.

I am going to give you the highlights, the main points, and I want you to think about them, flesh them out, and allow the Holy Spirit to give you further revelation.

Due to the nature of each one of these mandates, you are going to require a different kind of training. While you are going through them, you may start to understand why the Lord shifted you here and there.

He was suddenly establishing in you character traits or spiritual gifts that you did not have before. The trainings are going to be different - a different price is also going to be required for each.

Have you ever asked yourself, "How come I have to pay this price, and that guy does not have to pay this price?"

Certainly we see that with everybody else in the Church, but you see it as well from apostle to apostle. You look at other apostles, who have the same call, and you think, "How come they did not have to give that up?"

PAYING THE PRICE

I can imagine that this is how Paul must have felt when he said, "Hey guys, what is the deal? Peter gets to have a wife with him, the other apostles get to travel, but who are we? We are just nobodies. They can do what we cannot do." (1 Corinthians 5:5)

I do not think there are any of us who have an apostolic call who have not been there.

"Really, Lord, it is not fair. How come I have to pay that price, and they do not have to pay that price?"

It is because they are paying a price of their own. They are saying the exact same thing about you! Every mandate is different, and a different price is required for each. Each requires a different character.

Have you recognized the shaping of your character as a person?

Some people want to call it a paradigm shift. I call it character training. This is where the Lord will make you from one person into the next. It is miraculous. There is nothing that you can do with your own strength to make this happen.

MANDATES ARE PROGRESSIVE

There is something else that you need to realize. You can fulfill more than one mandate. In other words, you can complete one mandate and then move onto another. It is indeed progressive.

Another thing that you need to keep in mind is that this is a commission by God. You do not choose your mandate. Your mandate chooses you. As I go through each of these, you may say, "Being a David sounds nice. I wish I was a David."

Tough! God called you to be a Moses. What are you going to do about it?

"I want to be a Moses, like him."

"I want to be a David."

I am sorry, but there are some things that are written in stone, and this is one of those things. God, the Father, is the one who calls. Jesus set in the Church the prophets, apostles, and the rest of the fivefold ministry. (Ephesians 4:11)

He is the one who calls, commissions, and releases you. You do not pick this for yourself. You were born for this. You were created for this. Even Apostle Paul said that he was called in his mother's womb. (Galatians 1:15)

When you get that memo, firstly, you can let your ideas go. Then, you can come to peace, realizing that God has got this. God has always had this.

> *You do not need to panic that you are going to lose your calling. How can you lose something that you never had?*

If you are trying to hold onto something that is not your call, how can you lose something that you never held in your hand? If you do hold it in your hand, then you can rest assured that God Himself put it in your hand, and satan cannot snatch it from you.

Come to peace. You keep thinking that you are going to miss God, that you are going to miss Him and not fulfill your call or do what He told you to do.

You were literally born for this. You were created for this. Your spiritual and physical DNA was shaped for this. If you do not have the calling, it means you were not born for it.

God has already given you everything that you need. Come to peace, and let's get on with business. Let's discover what your calling is so that you can start walking it out.

APOSTOLIC MANDATES USING NEW TESTAMENT EXAMPLES AND OLD TESTAMENT TYPES

CHAPTER 21 – APOSTOLIC MANDATES USING NEW TESTAMENT EXAMPLES AND OLD TESTAMENT TYPES

Let's look at the apostolic mandates I referred to in the previous chapter. I am going to use some New Testament examples, and some Old Testament types, side by side. I have done teaching on each of these types separately, but I don't want to look so much at the types as I do the mandates that they fulfill.

1. SPIRITUAL PARENTS: PAUL AND ABRAHAM AND SARAH

The first type is the spiritual parenting mandate. Some fantastic examples of this are Peter and Paul, in the New Testament, and Abraham and Sarah, in the Old Testament.

Spiritual parenting is something that is becoming very popular in the Church right now. God is reviving spiritual mothers and fathers to re-parent the flock. We have a generation of orphans, broken men and women in the Church.

From the way society has been to the wrong choices parents have made, we have a lot of brokenness in the Church. God is raising up Abrahams and Sarahs to raise up these broken orphans, equip them, and send them out again.

I am going to read a passage here that defines Abraham and God's promise to him. I want you to see the price that he paid to fulfill that call.

LAYING IT OUT

Remember I told you that I want you to keep in mind the different trainings and the price each one pays.

Genesis 12:1 Now the Lord had said to Abram: "Get out of your country, from your family and from your father's house, to a land that I will show you.

2 I will make you a great nation; I will bless you and make your name great; and you shall be a blessing.

3 I will bless those who bless you, and I will curse him who curses you; and in you all the families of the earth shall be blessed."

I love the blessing part... but so many skim over the first part, don't they?

Abraham paid quite a price to fulfill this mandate. We are looking here at an apostle who is called to be a spiritual father - a patriarch. This is somebody who starts something new - one who originates a new tribe.

I talk a lot about tribes in the next book in this series, *Apostolic Teamwork*. A spiritual parent is somebody who begins a whole new spiritual DNA, if you will. I need you to realize something. Not every apostle is the same. I am talking about six types for now. I am sure that there are even more.

Perhaps you have even had a revelation of some. For me, these are the six that I have personally lived and that the Lord has shown us, so I am sharing them with you. One of the first is that of a spiritual parent.

Not every apostle is called to be an Abraham. Get the memo because you have these rising up in the kingdom of God right now, true apostles of God, and you are expecting them to be something that they will never be.

NOT EVERY APOSTLE IS A FATHER

There are some that you are wanting to be spiritual fathers, but they were never meant to be one. You are putting this expectation on them and getting disappointed when they do not pay up.

If God has not called you to be a spiritual father, you are trying to be something that you are not. It is discouraging for both sides.

So, let's identify your mandate and focus just on that. Like I said, God can shift you. Once you complete one mandate, He can take you to another. However, let's look at where you are at right now.

RAISES SPIRITUAL SONS

A spiritual father is one that raises up spiritual sons. This is why Peter and Paul are fantastic examples of this as well, especially Paul who raised up Timothy, Silas, and Titus. (1 Tim 1:2, Titus 1:4)

He was one who did not just teach the Word, but raised up sons who continued the work long after he left. A lot of the other disciples did not do this. They had different mandates.

Peter had John Mark, from what we can see in the Scriptures. John had a disciple that continued, according to history. You even have Polycarp in there who was a couple of generations down, but that is church history.

From what we can read, in the Word, there were very few that were fathers. We just assume that an apostle is a spiritual father, but it is not true. It may not be your mandate.

So, if you are not a spiritual father, take a deep breath. Maybe God is not calling you to be one. There are a couple of other types that you may be able to identify with. Not every apostle is called to be a spiritual parent, let it go.

However, if that is something that burns in you, and something that God has been doing in your life, then it is time to begin looking at it and realize that God is calling you to establish a new family.

THE PRICE OF SPIRITUAL PARENTING

Make no mistake. This comes with one of the highest prices of all the apostolic types. What does it mean to start a new spiritual DNA? The answer to this was in verse 1.

You must get out of your country, from your family and from your father's house, to a land that He shows you. In other words, you go to who knows where and leave everything that you know, everyone that you know, every spiritual DNA that you had, and everything that you received.

You leave behind every archetype, the food you ate, and the people you knew. You leave that country completely and become someone completely new.

If God is calling you to be a spiritual father, you do not get to stay at home. You do not get to keep what is familiar. You do not get to keep your nation, archetype, and family.

If God has called you to be an Abraham, make no mistake, there is a price that comes with it. Yet, not everyone is called to be an Abraham. We make this mistake of imposing our mandates on others.

Just because God asked you to give up your country, this does not mean that every apostle is asked to give up their country.

Some may just need to give up their state. Maybe they just need to move within the country.

There is certainly a lot of shifting around. When God calls you to be an apostle, I promise you, you should not get comfortable, because there will be a shifting. You will be changed.

However, not everybody is called to the same dramatic shift as Abraham or Paul were. Paul was sent from the Pharisees to the Gentiles. This was a complete shift. James did not have to pay that price.

Each apostolic mandate requires a different price.

---

2. PATTERN MAKERS: PAUL AND MOSES

Next, we have mandate number two. I call this apostle the pattern maker. I had this very incorrect notion. I thought that all apostles should be pattern makers.

When somebody did not know how to make a pattern, I thought, "You are not much of an apostle." I did not realize that there was more to being an apostle than just someone who evangelized and made patterns.

This is just one type of apostle. I think you are going to know pretty clearly who the New Testament example and Old Testament types are.

We will be looking again at Apostle Paul, but our Old Testament type is Moses, the ultimate pattern maker.

> *Exodus 25:9 According to all that I show you, that is, the pattern of the tabernacle and the pattern of all its furnishings, just so you shall make it.*

"Moses, I am going to give you the pattern for the tabernacle, the furnishings, everything. However, it will be just so that you will make it. You will make it exactly to spec. You are not going to add an extra ring where a ring should not be or a cubit where a cubit should not be. It will be exactly as I tell you to do it."

For one who is a pattern maker, I know that they have this kind of attention to detail. It should be just so. They are annoying. They are fussy, picky, and detail-oriented. It has to be just so.

What did you expect? They are pattern makers. What kind of training do you think a pattern maker has to go through?

For someone like me, I had to go through a lot of training because I am not analytical, and I do not like thinking about details. I just want to run and do, hop, skip, jump, pick up my sword, and fight bad guys. That is me.

Becoming a pattern maker was the hardest season of my life because I had to do something that I had never done before. I had to think, in detail, and put the pieces together as God gave them to me.

Not everyone can get the pattern. Even as I go through each of these mandates, I want you to already start seeing how possible it is for apostles to work together. Not everybody can be a spiritual parent, and not everybody can be a pattern maker.

However, you can certainly work together toward the same goal, can't you?

Absolutely! It is because you are going to have different functions in the Church. The goal is the same, but how you will walk it out is going to be different for each apostle. You are going to start seeing how it is possible to start bringing unity in the body of Christ.

For each of the apostles, in the New Testament, you saw how they had their own mandate. Yet, you see how they did join together. You see how Timothy, Silas, and Paul got together, and they could work as apostles together. (1 Thessalonians 1:1 is an example of this teamwork, having penned this Epistle together.)

It is possible. I know that right now we are not seeing it in the Church. The only way we see apostles working together in today's day and age is through ministry association. You know, "I rub shoulders with you. You rub shoulders with me."

"I know Apostle Superstar. Yes, he is my good friend and buddy."

APOSTLES SIDE BY SIDE

They use these relationships so that they sound really good. That is the only way we really see apostles working together today. However, a time is coming, a change is coming, where God will call His apostles to work together to build the End-Times Church.

We cannot do it alone. Each of us has different mandates and visions. However, if you bring it all together, you will get the full picture. No one apostle has the full picture. Even in the New Testament, there was not one great man of God who had the full picture.

Also, in the Old Testament, although Moses got a large part of it, we see how the judges and kings come along, and God even added to what Moses did. Not even Moses had the fullness of understanding. God added to it through the years.

It is the same with us. You cannot be a solo player here.

It is time that we each recognize our place and acknowledge the place of others, and have some humility and readiness to listen and serve one another in love.

Guys, this is something that we do not see in the Church. Can we change it in our hearts? Can we take the first step forward in the right direction? Can we build those patterns?

YOU MIGHT NOT BUILD

This is something that you need to realize as well. Just because you are a pattern maker, this does not mean that you get to build the pattern. Look at David. He got the pattern for the temple, and he was so excited about it.

He was ready to build and God said, "No, you will not build it." (2 Samuel 7)

His eyes never saw the glory of the temple of Solomon. We misunderstand that sometimes. God has called you to get the pattern. Often times, that means that He needs someone else to build it because you need to continue seeking Him for more patterns, because you are a pattern maker.

More patterns are required for more works. If that is your mandate, then God will always give you patterns. He will give you patterns for different things and visions, and it will evolve.

If you try to build and get the pattern, you will stretch yourself out way too thin. You cannot do both at the same time. Even when Moses got the pattern, he did not build the tabernacle.

He got the pattern for it, but the Lord told him exactly who should be involved in the building of it. Others built it, but he went up the mountain again and again to get the pattern so that they could build. Each one of us has a place to belong. (Exodus 31)

The pattern maker is one who does a new thing.
He creates a pattern and a way of doing things
that we did not know before. He is an originator.

Not every apostle is an originator, nor do they need to be one. That is only mandate number two.

We have to realize that there is a lot of diversity that God has set in His Church. There was always diversity. If you look in the Scriptures, you can see the diversity from Genesis to Revelation. We just have not taken time to really look at it.

We have not taken time to see how vital each part is.

3. TRAILBLAZERS: PETER AND JOSHUA

The third apostolic type is what I like to call the trailblazer. In my opinion, this is the most fun of all the apostolic types. The New Testament example of this is Peter, and the Old Testament type is Joshua.

> *Exodus 17:10 So Joshua did as Moses said to him, and fought with Amalek. And Moses, Aaron, and Hur went up to the top of the hill.*

There was Moses at the top of the hill, bored to death saying, "Yeah... go boys."

Where was Joshua?

He was down in the trenches with a sword in his hand, taking the land for God's people. He was in battle. Moses did not have to be in battle. He was the pattern maker. It was smart for him to stay up on the hill.

Plus, he was getting a little old. He was a little tired. He could not even keep his arms up the whole time. He needed Aaron and Hur to keep his arms up. I think it made sense for him to stay up on top of the mountain, because if he was taken out, who would have finished the pattern?

He got more than just the pattern for the tabernacle, remember? He got more than just the law and the precepts.

He also got the pattern for how to divide the land between all the tribes. There was a lot of patterns that he got in his lifetime. It was a good idea that he did not die quite yet. However, there was somebody who did need to go and take the land, blaze a trail, and go where angels feared to tread.

PETER BLAZES A TRAIL

This was much like Apostle Peter. I call him the trailblazer because he was the first to step into a Gentile home and bring salvation to the Gentiles.

He broke a barrier, a social and religious barrier, that no one had ever broken before.

He stepped into the unknown and unexpected and did what everybody thought was the worst thing to possibly do. He went and ate, fellowshipped, and stepped into the home of a Gentile. He broke the veil and tore it right down the middle.

> *That is what the trailblazer is called to do. He goes*
> *ahead, having the courage to go where angels*
> *fear to tread, with his sword held high. He breaks*
> *those barriers, gets into people's faces, and*
> *smashes mindsets.*

They are the ones with the sharp edge and are full of foolishness. They are the ones like Peter who got into Jesus' face saying, "That is not going to happen to you."

"Get behind me, satan."

Sometimes they cannot tell if satan is driving them, their flesh is driving them, or if the Holy Spirit is driving them. They are all over the place sometimes.

What a different character from Moses. Moses is a thinker. He is putting the pattern together. He has patience because the Lord knows, he climbed up that mountain so many times. To do that, you need patience.

Then, you have Joshua. He was so fiery. He stayed in the presence of the Lord longer than Moses did.

Joshua 1:3 says "Everywhere you place your feet, I have given it to you."

He had boldness and courage. He stepped out with his sword in hand. We need those trailblazers. They tend to be very evangelistic. They go into the worst places.

You can fulfill more than one mandate, but if you are the pattern maker, then you need yourself a Joshua. Are you starting to see how the apostles work together yet? Do you see that you do not have to do it by yourself?

The biggest mistake that you can make is to try and be all of these by yourself. I know this because I have been there. It is impossible. You cannot stand at the top of the hill, getting the pattern, and then hop and jump down the hill, pick up a sword, and fight the enemy at the same time.

What is it going to be? What is it that God is calling you to do?

You know the job that needs to be done, but you can only do the job that you are called to do. You can only fulfill the mandate that God has put on your life. You cannot fulfill someone else's mandate.

That is why we need one another. More often than not, God will send a Joshua ahead of you to go and break the hard ground to prepare the way, upset people, and unsettle the status quo so that you can come with a pattern, and they will be ready for the pattern when it is time.

Had Joshua not taken the land, how could they have established the kingdom? We need the trailblazers. We need the Peters who had the courage to step in. Look at what happened.

PAUL AND PETER – WHAT A TEAM!

Had Peter not taken that step forward for the Gentiles and spiritually and physically unlocked the realm of heaven for the Gentiles with his key, where would Paul be today?

You see, Paul was our pattern maker. He needed to bring that pattern to the Church. Where would we be today though, if Peter was not obedient to the voice of God? The Church would not have realized that salvation was for the Gentiles also.

He broke barriers. He went where no one else had gone. We need such trailblazers again. However, what are we doing? We are tying them down and telling them to behave and be nice, quiet little girls and boys.

We have the pattern makers and spiritual parents, and the trailblazers keep upsetting the status quo. That is their mandate. They are meant to break ground.

They are the kind that will go into a territory. They may even start a couple of churches. They will start something completely new, break the ground, and then leave. You think, "What kind of person is that?"

It sounds like a Joshua to me. It sounds like a trailblazer, someone that goes ahead. We just need another apostle to follow that work up with a pattern, so that something can truly be built.

THE NATURE OF TRAILBLAZERS

These are men of war. With the nature of this apostolic mandate, this is one that is going to include a lot of spiritual warfare. You will be doing warfare at the highest level. There will be backlashes, demon manifestations, nasty words, and words spoken against you.

This is not an easy mandate, but it really is the most fun. You get to shout, scream, upset people, go ahead, break new ground, go into new territories, challenge new archetypes, and challenge denominations.

For everybody who is called to that mandate, you know that it can be a lot of fun. It is only fun if you are called to it though. Everyone else is like… "Why?"

"I just wanted a nice afternoon tea. We were going to sit down with the leaders and fellowship with the Lord and have a nice time. However, you invited a Joshua." What did you expect?

The fire is going to come because they have a hard edge and a sword that has been sharpened over years and years of use.

We need each other. You cannot be a Moses and a Joshua at the same time. You can move from one to the other. I started out as a Joshua actually. I broke the ground when the ministry first started.

Craig and I were both Joshuas together, side by side. When the opportunity came, we were the first ones to go to Europe. We went where angels fear to tread. We did not even know many there.

We were the first to go and start the works, challenge the people, and get them inspired.

If I look back, to be honest, I am a little embarrassed because I had a great amount of zeal, but very little wisdom and knowledge. We were very young and ambitious. We were going to change the world *tomorrow*.

We were Joshuas, and that is the nature of one who is such. We did spiritual warfare. We went from region to region, declaring and decreeing, releasing decrees in the spirit. We were upsetting people and having the time of our lives. It was tough, but it was fun.

When my father handed the ministry over to Craig and I, I was so ready to be Joshua again. I was so used to going ahead and breaking ground. Then, he would follow after and do the teaching and pattern making.

God said, "You know you have to be Moses now, right?"

"That means I have to stand on top of the mountain, Lord?"

"Yes. That is exactly what it means, and someone else will do the fighting now."

NAVIGATING THE TRANSITIONS

You can shift mandates, but it meant a character change for me. It meant that I had to go through a process. When God has had you in one of these, he will take you through a transitional season to move onto the next because you have to finish one first before you can go onto the next.

You have to make sure that you complete that mandate, and I did complete that mandate. Actually, when I look back today, I look and see exactly what that accomplished, because now we have ministry centers in all those places.

Through the years, God actually used those seeds that we sowed back then. The ground that we broke back then, we are building on now. We need each one of these mandates in the Church today.

TRAINERS, BUILDERS AND FINISHERS

CHAPTER 22 – TRAINERS, BUILDERS AND FINISHERS

4. TRAINERS: JESUS, PAUL AND DAVID

Then, we have our fourth mandate. I like to call these the trainers. For a New Testament example, I have Jesus, who I could have put on every one of the Apostolic Types because He fulfilled every one!

However, I really love how He worked with His twelve Disciples specifically, so I wanted to focus on that for this particular apostolic type.

Of course, Paul was another one that was a trainer. I could even list more of the disciples. You can see how they moved from one to the other as they matured and got more wisdom as the Lord trained them further.

> *Acts 19:9 But when some were hardened and did not believe, but spoke evil of the Way before the multitude, he departed from them and withdrew the disciples, reasoning daily in the school of Tyrannus.*
>
> *10 And this continued for two years, so that all who dwelt in Asia heard the word of the Lord Jesus, both Jews and Greeks.*

I see such a sudden shift in Paul's ministry. He now sits and trains for a couple of years. Is that not what Jesus did as well with His twelve Disciples?

He took three years to train them. I love the example of our Old Testament type, who is David. What a fantastic example of a trainer. He took those mighty warriors, got their strengths, banded them together, and made them a unique and powerful force for the kingdom of Israel.

TRAINER OF MIGHTY MEN

He was a trainer of mighty men. This apostolic type trains up leaders and believers to do good works of every kind. Now, I want you to understand something. He is not just a teacher. He is a trainer - an equipper.

This is another action word. Moses, although a pattern maker, is also a really good teacher and spiritual father. You will notice how each one of these apostolic mandates include a bit of all of the fivefold ministry.

There may be more of a teaching orientation, evangelistic, or prophetic, but I am going way beyond that. I am looking at your commission as a whole. How you will fulfill your commission will differ from apostle to apostle.

However, I am looking at this commission that God is giving each of us to fulfill. David is a fantastic picture of a trainer. He banded the mighty men together. Look at Paul. He trained up the elders and apostles.

Consider Paul's spiritual sons - he did not just parent them, but he trained them to do the job so that he could leave them behind or send them ahead to handle things.

You are going to find these guys start prophetic schools, not just Bible schools. You are looking at people who are training up intercessors, teaching them hands on. They are teaching people how to pray or how to evangelize.

"Let me show you. Come on the streets with me. Let's evangelize together."

This is somebody who is a trainer - an equipper. They are not just teachers. Yes, teaching will be involved. You cannot train without doing some teaching, but your main focus again is a "doing word".

"Let's do the job. Let me show you how to do the job."

THAT TRAINER "EYE"

When you are a trainer, you are very focused on what you do. When you are working with someone, you will always see the flaws. I know that I am dealing with a trainer when all they see is what needs to change.

Of course they see that. They are like a personal life coach who says, "If you want to be a success, we need to deal with that poverty mentality, we need to change your hair cut, and we need to change your attitude. Let's work on this character of yours and make you successful."

> *That is what a trainer does. They push you to your limit so that the potential in you can come out. There are apostles whose passion is this focus.*

We get so much pressure from those around us. Fellow leaders, those who follow us, other believers in the Church, all trying to conform us to what everybody else is doing.

You can come under so much condemnation because you keep doing things so differently. Yet, you are an apostle. You are meant to be doing things differently. It is part and parcel of the call. It is our difference that unites us. It is our diversity that makes us strong.

God has put us in these positions for a reason. If you conform yourself to someone or something else, you will not be effective in the mandate that God has called you to do.

You will have one foot in one mandate and another foot in someone else's mandate. You will not move forward or backwards. You will be stuck in the mud - going nowhere fast.

If you want to move forward, you need to focus on the mandate that God has given you.

If you have been called to be a trainer, it is one of the most difficult mandates that there is.

It is a thankless job. It is a calling. No one can handle that much rebuff, rejection, failure, and people bailing out on them, without it being a call.

I look at what so many of my team go through as trainers in our ministry. The hours, the days, the years that they travail with each one of their students and disciples. They cry over them, pray over them, and work day and night with them.

They do all of this, and for many of the students, when the going gets tough, they just turn around and say, "I am done. I cannot do this. I am out of here. I do not need to take that from you. I do not need to take that correction. I do not need to hear that I need to deal with my sin. I do not have any sin. I do not need to deal with that."

Do you know how much courage it takes to get into someone's face and say, "You are full of bitterness and pride. Die already!"

Do you know how much courage it takes when you know the rebuff that you are going to get?

"Sorry, that word is a spirit of divination. You are in complete deception, you are demonized, and you need to deal with that."

People just love hearing that all the time. They love it when you tell them that. It is their favorite thing to hear...

However, it is unavoidable when you are training prophets, who thought that it would be a good idea to look for the spirit of God in places where they should have never gone looking.

They start "activating" certain things in their spirit that really do not need any activating at all. They were not exactly activated by the Holy Spirit either (if you know what I am saying).

They were born with generational bondages of a spirit of divination, and then they try to bring that into prophetic ministry. You know what I am talking about. We see this rampant in the Church right now.

Said Simply: That is a Demon!

Why is it rampant in the Church? It is because no one has the courage to get in their faces and say, "That is a demon." However, a trainer does, and they are prepared for the backlash. Yet, that does not mean it is easy.

Of course, this is not easy. Who likes to be spewed at and told that they are a dominating leader, trying to push their agenda on them? They tell you that you do not know anything and that you do not know the price they paid to get what they have.

They go as far as saying, "What will I be without this?"

No one in their right mind wants to face that kind of opposition. However, when you are a trainer, you have the courage for that. You have the courage to get up again and again and face it again and again.

I take my hat off to those in my team who are such trainers. They take more rebuff, backlashes, and bitter words than you can imagine as the students are going through training.

When we have our graduations, each trainer cries because they know the journey that each student has gone on. When I cry, however, I cry for my trainers because I remember the price that they paid to get each student there.

I remember sitting around the dinner table talking about each student with my trainers, and how they wonder if their students are going to make it through.

I remember sitting and praying them through when they came to cry on my shoulder, saying, "I have obviously failed. I am the worst trainer ever. What have I done wrong? What do I need to do? Where should I go next?"

This is what I remember when each graduate stands up on that stage. I look at the price that each one of them has paid to put you there. That is the heart of a trainer. When you have that heart, only the Holy Spirit could have put it there.

WE NEED MORE DAVIDS

No one can take that much punishment just for the fun of it. We need more Davids in the Church who have the courage to go through with God's people.

We even have some who have the courage to get in your face and say that you have a demon, but how many have the courage to take you by the scruff of your neck and deal with it until the demon is gone?

Who is going to deal with the spewing, bitterness, and garbage until the demon is gone? How many people have the courage to go through with you after they have made you manifest?

Not a whole lot. That is why we need more trainers in the body of Christ. If you are a trainer, then please stop trying to be a pattern maker. Trainers are the worst pattern makers because their pattern is all about changing everything.

They go on and on telling everyone what to change and that they need to "die already". What are you going to build? You are always spending time tearing things down. They are terrible pattern makers.

Pattern makers, you make the worst trainers as well.

Moses says, "Let's structure it, and make sure that this does not happen again."

David says, "I do not have time to do that right now. There is a demon to deal with here, a life to change, and some equipping to do."

> *Each one of us has a place. Find your place, and recognize that this is a mandate from the Father, an honor and privilege. If you are looking for a position and a title, here it is right here, bundled in with the price that you are called to pay for it.*

5. BUILDERS: JAMES AND SOLOMON

The fifth mandate I like to call the builders. I think the builders probably have the best work satisfaction, because they get to see the finished product. The Old Testament type is Solomon, as you can imagine. The New Testament example is James, Jesus' brother, the apostle in Jerusalem.

I love the book of James. A lot of people do not understand the book of James, but I get James. This was his mandate. He was a builder. You have Peter with his big mouth, breaking ground, and Paul getting his patterns and laying out the structure.

Take a look at all the patterns that Paul set for the New Testament Church. Where would we be as a Body without that pattern?

He set us up on how we should be prophesying, the gifts of the Spirit, the hierarchy of the fivefold ministry. He laid every pattern for marriage and Christianity. For so many different aspects of our Christian walk, we really needed it.

Then, there was somebody who had to make all of this happen. It is one thing to have a pattern, but then you need somebody to live with it. Paul did so much moving around. He was maybe two years here, and maybe three years there.

For the most part, he did a circuit, and he was always moving around. How can you build when you never stay in one place long enough?

Look at David. He did the same thing. He was all over the place. He was always going out for war. When he stayed home... we know how that worked out for him. It is not good to leave a David at home. He gets up to way too much "hanky panky." Send the man out to war!

SOLOMON AND JAMES

> *1 Chronicles 22:10 He shall build a house for My name, and he shall be My son, and I will be his Father; and I will establish the throne of his kingdom over Israel forever.*

I also love this illustration of James in Galatians 2. Paul is explaining what happened when he had been running the race a bit.

He had been sent to the Gentiles, and he was getting all these patterns and thought, "Maybe I should go and hang out with some of the other apostles and find out if this race has been in vain. I am pretty sure I am on track, but let me go and see if I am really on track."

Who did he go and visit?

> *Galatians 2:9 and when James, Cephas, and John, who seemed to be pillars, perceived the grace that had been given to me, they gave me and Barnabas the right hand of fellowship, that we should go to the Gentiles and they to the circumcised.*

James stayed at home to build. He built the church at Jerusalem. He paid his life for the church at Jerusalem. It became this hub, where even those from the center in Antioch visited to make sure that they were still on track.

Sure there were some things about James that caused conflicts. He was a good Jew, and there came some conflicts between how the church at Antioch was built and how Jerusalem was built.

However, I still love the illustration of James. When you read the book of James, you get the man.

"Guys, this is how you are behaving in your fellowship. You are acting like a bunch of children. You are busy striving for your pleasures and bickering amongst one another." (James 4)

I am like, "James, were you just at one of the church meetings down the road the other night?"

"Where is this striving and conflict coming from among you? Your desires for pleasure that strive within your members. You lust and do not obtain. You murder and covet, yet you do not have. You do not have because you do not ask. When you do ask, you ask amiss, just for your own pleasures."

I could have preached that last Sunday, right?

THE PASTOR'S PASTOR

This is a man who knew what it was like to live at the local church every single day. He was a pastor's pastor. He lived with the people every day. He did not just talk about patterns. He lived the patterns and made them very practical for the people to follow.

If you are called to be a James or a Solomon, then you are called to build. That means that you are called to stay at home.

I know that an apostle is one who is sent, and certainly James was sent, commissioned by Jesus Himself. However, we always think that this means we are going to leave the country.

Remember what I shared for the spiritual parent? They have to leave country and family. However, it is not so with James. James stayed at home. He stayed there and took care of business.

He built up and established the work right there. If you would just stop for a minute, you would see that we already have a lot of James' in the body of Christ right now.

We love to knock those bishops, and I am first in line for that.

"Really, have you just not got the courage to call yourself an apostle? You think that wearing a collar and calling yourself a bishop, instead of apostle, is giving you a bit of a foot in the door?"

These are the James'. There is nothing wrong with that. We need them. We need those that stay at home to build. Not everybody can go out. Who is going to stay at home in Jerusalem and be that covering and place of warmth?

The rest of the apostles, who have been going out, need a place where they can come and find shelter. Actually, Peter was one of the elders in the church of Jerusalem, but he was never at home.

Peter was out there blazing trails everywhere he went. He was always breaking ground, going out, healing the sick, spreading the gospel – moving, going and fighting. Afterwards, he needed to come home, to a place of refuge.

A PLACE TO BELONG

He came home to Jerusalem. That is where James was keeping the campfire burning. We need the James' who will build the pattern and establish it. They need to build a place of comfort, a place where people can belong.

If God keeps grounding you and not letting you go out but keeps telling you to build, then maybe you are a Solomon or James and are meant to be hands on. You are practical, and you are going to teach, instruct, and get involved day by day.

This is not for everyone. If you are not a Solomon or James, do not feel guilty because you are not one. You are not meant to be one. I think this is the most common apostolic type that we see in the Church right now. So, everyone thinks that this is what it is supposed to be like.

I consider Jesus. What church did He build? Where were His steeples? Where was His congregation?

I did not see a building, a big church that He established by the time that He died. Yet, He started a movement that we are still part of today. Not all of us can be a James. Some of us have to go out.

Just because you have not built a big church does not mean that you are not an apostle. This just means that you are not a James.

If you are meant to be a James though, then it is time for you to begin to build. You need to take the pattern and establish it. You may not receive the pattern, but you sure know how to take the pattern and make it into what it should look like.

ROCK THE PATTERN!

Look at Solomon. He did not get the pattern, but what he did with that pattern was amazing. He made it shine. He rocked that pattern. I love that. Even in our ministry, with me being the pattern maker, I think that I have it all together. I say, "This is how we are going to do it."

Then, one of the Solomons in my team get a hold of that pattern, and they put bling all over it. They bling it and make it all extravagant. They are builders. That is what they do. They are like, "I am going to bedazzle this pattern. Check this out!"

That is what they are supposed to do. They make it look good. Solomon did not just build the temple. He built so much more than that. He built his palace and cities, and he took the land by building on it.

David also took the land, but he took it with the tip of a sword. Solomon took the land in a very different way. He established it by building on it, and making sure that the children of Israel could not be rooted up from it very easily.

6. THE FINISHER – TIMOTHY AND AARON

For our last apostolic type, we have who I call, the finishers. Our New Testament example is Timothy, and our Old Testament type is Aaron.

> *1 Corinthians 4:17 For this reason I have sent Timothy to you, who is my beloved and faithful son in the Lord, who will remind you of my ways in Christ, as I teach everywhere in every church.*

> **Numbers 3:8** *Also they shall attend to all the furnishings of the tabernacle of meeting, and to the needs of the children of Israel, to do the work of the tabernacle.*
>
> *9 And you shall give the Levites to Aaron and his sons; they are given entirely to him from among the children of Israel.*

Moses got the picture, the pattern. You have Paul who got the pattern as well. Yet, I love 1 Corinthians 4 above, where it says that Timothy, his son, will remind them of Paul's ways in Christ.

When Paul is sent to be beheaded, Timothy is still finishing the work that Paul started. It is just like how Aaron took the pattern that Moses had begun, and from generation to generation, continued the work.

Even long after the tabernacle had been exchanged for a temple, we still see the sons of Aaron continuing the work. They worked side by side with Moses. Aaron is one that may not get the pattern, but he is certainly the one that sees it to the end and continues it.

He is the finisher. He makes sure that the job gets done. He is very pastoral and hands on, with a heart for the people. He gets involved. He takes the pattern that has been given to him and makes sure that it is finished to the end.

He makes sure that the light fixtures are on, and the finishing touches are on. He does not just build. He completes the building completely. This takes a lot of pressure off you, if you are called to be an Aaron or Timothy. You do not have to be the trailblazer.

You do not have to get a pattern, and you do not even have to be a spiritual parent. You just have to make sure that the job gets finished. Is the mandate completed?

I am sure that you know some people who walk in that anointing. They are finishers. You get your starters, and you get your finishers. Timothy and Aaron have a patience to see it through to the end.

As a gift, they get to enter into the Holy of Holies – something that not even Moses did. It was not the sons of Moses but the sons of Aaron that were remembered from generation to generation. The work of Aaron is often thankless, but because of the price that he was willing to pay to take second place, he is put to the front of the line!

Aaron followed his younger brother, giving that place of honor that belonged to him away. Yet God remembered him and so gave him a place Moses did not have. As an Aaron, it burns in you to take the pattern to the next generation.

You want to do more than see a temple built - you want to see it established in the heart's of God's people. You come down from the pulpit and work day by day with each one that comes to you, building the truth into their hearts. Just like Timothy, your work is "nitty gritty", and you will go where the temple is!

You are also one to stay at home, but the Lord will shift you at first. Neither Aaron or Timothy were allowed to stay where they were born. Rather they were moved into place. Timothy's father was a Greek, and Aaron had to leave Egypt to find his place.

However, when they found their place, they settled there and built the pattern.

Moses is the one who gets the pattern and then hands it out to the builders so that they might build it. They will work with the finishers, who will see it through to the end and passed on to the next generation. What an incredible team we are, working together, hand in hand.

Can you see how the apostles can work together?

Some are going to blaze a trail, some are going to build the Church, and some are going to get the pattern. Together, we are going to establish the kingdom of God.

> *1 Corinthians 3:6* *I planted, Apollos watered, but God gave the increase.*

One sows, and another waters. Is this not what Apostle Paul was talking about? One lays a foundation, and another builds on it. One gets a pattern, the next breaks ground, the next builds, the next maintains, the next equips and trains for function within it.

Each one of us has our place, and our part to play. We can work together to do it, if we have some humility and are prepared to leave the "me, myself, and I" aside and just do what God has called us to do.

THE FUNCTIONS
OF THE APOSTLE

CHAPTER 23 – THE FUNCTIONS OF THE APOSTLE

In all of these six mandates that I have mentioned to you, there are nine very specific functions that they all fulfill. So, regardless of what your mandate is, you should fulfill these.

What are you - a builder, a finisher, a trainer, a pattern maker?

Now that you know what your job is, how do you know if you are doing your job?

These are just nine points for now. I hope that you add to these. I want to challenge you. Do not just be like baby birds. Fly like eagles for yourselves and get your own revelation please.

> ***Ephesians 4:11*** *And He Himself gave some to be apostles, some prophets, some evangelists, and some pastors and teachers,*
>
> *12 for the equipping of the saints for the work of ministry, for the edifying of the body of Christ,*
>
> *13 till we all come to the unity of the faith and of the knowledge of the Son of God, to a perfect man, to the measure of the stature of the fullness of Christ;*

1. TO RECEIVE A MANDATE AND IMPLEMENT IT

> ***2 Timothy 3:10*** *But you have carefully followed my doctrine, manner of life, purpose, faith, longsuffering, love, perseverance,*

How can you even fulfill your mandate when you do not know what it is?

Let's start with step one, get a mandate, or should I rather say, recognize your mandate. You cannot go and get a mandate because God gives us a mandate. It is like I said with a vision. You cannot just catch it.

No one is throwing a mandate at you that you can catch. You receive one from the Holy Spirit. So, number one is to recognize your mandate and begin implementing it.

2. To Equip the Leaders Within that Mandate

The next thing that you need to do is equip the leaders within that mandate. You know who you are. Obviously, with this mandate in place, God has already brought those to you that share aspects and visions within that mandate.

Are you equipping them for it, or are you just worrying about yourself?

> ***2 Timothy 4:1*** *I charge you therefore before God and the Lord Jesus Christ, who will judge the living and the dead at His appearing and His kingdom:*
>
> *2 Preach the word! Be ready in season and out of season. Convince, rebuke, exhort, with all longsuffering and teaching.*

Paul is instructing Timothy. He did not just give Timothy the pattern. He trained him in it. He equipped him in the pattern. Do not just throw a pattern at someone and expect that they suddenly know how to build it, finish it, or do anything with it.

Paul laid it out very clearly. Have you equipped the leaders?

David positioned his mighty men. Moses imparted the anointing that was on him to the seventy elders. Paul raised up Timothy and Silas.

So what, you have a mandate... big deal!

Who is running with you?

Have you taken time to raise up those who are going to fulfill it with you?

3. To Establish Structure

If you are an apostle, you should have established a structure. This is another function that you should be fulfilling in the church. If you call yourself an apostle, I want to know what your mandate is, I want to see the fruit of that in those that you have raised up, and I want to see your structure.

> *2 Timothy 1:13 Hold fast the pattern of sound words which you have heard from me, in faith and love which are in Christ Jesus.*

> *1 Corinthians 14:39 Therefore, brethren, desire earnestly to prophesy, and do not forbid to speak with tongues.*

> *40 Let all things be done decently and in order.*

He did not just teach them about the spiritual gifts. He brought structure. Moses, Paul, James - they all gave structure. Even David, who was a trainer, had structure. What does your structure look like?

You need organization. I know that prophets often hate this. However, this is not a prophetic book, is it? This is an apostolic book. So, tell me, apostle, what does your structure look like?

4. To Drive the Vision Forward (Including Displacement)

You should be familiar with this next point. You need to drive the vision forward. This scripture epitomizes driving the vision forward.

> *Philippians 3:13 Brethren, I do not count myself to have apprehended; but one thing I do, forgetting those things which are behind and reaching forward to those things which are ahead,*

> *14 I press toward the goal for the prize of the upward call of God in Christ Jesus.*

I see Paul running a race, saying, "I forget those things that are behind, and I continue to press forward. I drive the vision forward. Those things that are behind me are past, over, and done. What is the next vision?"

An apostle is one who drives the vision forward. He is one who takes the Church through transition. He allows it to evolve. You have Joshua who took the children of Israel from the wilderness and into the Promised Land.

You have David who took the children of Israel from a divided kingdom into a united kingdom. You have Paul who took them from the Old Testament into the New Testament.

The apostle is one who takes the Church through transition because they drive the vision forward, and they continue to get revelation. You cannot just rip the old way away from them and take away the old vision.

You have to drive a vision forward and help the Church transition into it. If you are an apostle, what are you transitioning the Church into?

Even if you are a pattern maker, that means that you are displacing an old pattern. If you are a trainer, that means that you are teaching them a new way of doing things. If you are blazing a trail, of course, you are challenging old mindsets, status quo, doctrines, religion, and archetypes.

You know that there is a displacement going on, regardless of your mandate. You are driving it forward. What are you doing to transition the Church from the old to the new?

You cannot just wait for God to do it all by Himself. God chose you. You have to step forward and fulfill your function. Drive the vision forward.

5. TO CREATE A PLACE FOR MINISTRY

An apostle is not just one that starts a ministry. An apostle is one that creates a place for ministry.

Until Jesus had come along, there was no such thing as apostles. Until David came along there was no such thing as twenty-four-hour praise and worshippers, there were no mighty men, and certainly a prophet did not have a place in court.

David created a position for the seer. He created a position for the worshippers. Moses created a position for the seventy elders. He made something that was not there before.

We spoke about raising up the mighty men, but it is not good enough to just raise up the mighty men. Are you giving them a place to function in, once they are raised up? That is what an apostle does.

An apostle looks and says, "You do not have a place. Let's make you a custom fit place for your call. Holy Spirit, what do I do?"

Guess what happens when you do that, apostle? The work grows. You multiply. You do not have five mighty warriors that are all doing the same thing, in the same position, all left wondering why you are not getting anywhere.

No, you have five mighty warriors that you create a place for so that they can function in their unique calling.

SPECIFIC PLACEMENT

I was so focused on the Prophetic School at one time, because that was the birth of my ministry. That was what I started with.

When God started calling me to be a Moses, He said, "Your thinking is about to shift in a very big way. I am bringing you people with callings that you did not even know were callings.

They are going to have a heart to do things that you do not even consider ministry.

Yet, these things are ministries, and I have called them to do it. You better find a place for them. They will have a heart for the lost, for the elderly, to pray... all these diverse desires.

Don't you dare send them away, but instead, you need to create a place for them in your ministry. Establish a department just for them, so that they can flourish in it."

We are not seeing this in the Church or the apostolic ministry, but we need to see it more. We are too stuck in what we already know.

The Church is stuck in a thinking that says, "This is a calling, and these are the only positions we have available in the church."

We need to identify the potential in the mighty warriors and then create a place for them to function to the fullest of their potential.

An apostle is not one who talks about positions, but one who creates and custom fits a position to a mighty warrior.

---

6. TO APPOINT PEOPLE TO THEIR PLACE

> **Titus 1:5** *For this reason I left you in Crete, that you should set in order the things that are lacking, and appoint elders in every city as I commanded you*

The apostle is one who should be appointing people to positions, not just setting himself up.

Please Lord, save us from this self promotion!!

We got it already. We know that you are the apostle, the bishop, the senior pastor. We know who you are, but who is everyone else?

Servants, shepherds, sheep, I do not know... Can we start appointing others to do the job? Can we start appointing other apostles?

I know that there are some that are doing it, so I am not knocking all the apostles out there, just those that stand on their tower and keep all the glory to themselves. I am not too fond of those.

A huge part of our function is to appoint. Sometimes, God will send Craig and I to the most obscure places, just to go and appoint someone, put them in an office, and leave again.

He will send us to the middle of nowhere, to a little church or meeting, a sidetrack, to pick up a mighty warrior. We will go and appoint someone into apostolic office or prophetic office, and that is all He had us travel halfway around the world to do.

This has happened to us many times because the Lord needs His apostles to lay hands, impart, release, and place people in that office, and not a lot of them are doing it.

APOSTOLIC ORDINATION

Too often we are saying "ordinations" that go along the lines of, "You have been faithful to this ministry for a long time and have gone through our Bible school course, so we have decided that we are going to ordain you to be an apostle because you look very apostolic right now."

Shouldn't we ask God, the Father, what He wants?

What is this apostle's mandate? What is their structure, and where is their team?

They do not need you to qualify them. The Father qualifies them. Your part is to lay your hands, release the power, and walk away. They are an apostle. They will get the rest of this just fine.

Walk next to an apostle, not over him. If they are not fulfilling their function, then they are not apostles. They are just lackeys, but you gave them the title apostle so that they will stay in your ministry.

This is not the kind of "releasing" that I am talking about. That is not the function I am talking about when I say, "Appoint them to their place."

I am talking about releasing, decreeing, imparting, giving them the anointing and power, and confirming for them what God has already told them. Then, you send them and let the Holy Spirit send them out.

There may be some that will stay and walk alongside you. I have a few of those. Yet, for most of those that I have ordained and released into apostolic office, they went out to be apostles.

How about that?

They went off to do their mandate, their work, in their realm. That was the point. It was not for them to stay under me. I did not appoint them. God appointed them. We need to see a little bit more of this in the body of Christ.

7. To Impart the Power of God to Others

> **Romans 1:11** *For I long to see you, that I may impart to you some spiritual gift, so that you may be established*

The apostle, because of the nature of his training and his journey, has gone through a refining process. His vessel has been stretched from here to kingdom come. As a result, he has accumulated the authority, power, and anointing to do the work that God has called him to do.

What I love about this is that we went through all of that, not to hold onto it, but to impart it to others so that they can eat the fruit of our labor. They can take the shortcut. They do not have to go through that whole process that we went through.

The apostle is meant to impart the gifts. I love doing that. It is my favorite thing to do. If you have been through any of our schools, I did not even have to lay hands on you, but you got that gift of discerning of spirits, didn't you?

God does not mess around with that gift of discerning of spirits. That is probably one of the gifts that I flow in the strongest, so everybody always picks that up. You will not believe how many people got Spirit-filled and started speaking in tongues after going through some of our courses.

Just the impartation establishes them in their calling. I do not doubt that they could get it from the Lord on their own. Of course they can. However, it is nice to have a shortcut.

That is why the apostle is there. You have gone through the long journey so that others do not have to. An apostle is meant to be imparting and releasing. Maybe they are meant to stay, and maybe they are not.

Let's please impart the gifts and anointing that God's people need to overcome the problems in their lives and also to be established to do the work of God that He has called them to do.

8. To Reveal the Fullness of God to His People

> **Colossians 1:19** *For it pleased the Father that in Him all the fullness should dwell, 20 and by Him to reconcile all things to Himself, by Him, whether things on earth or things in heaven, having made peace through the blood of His cross.*

In my prophetic teachings, I speak about how the prophet reveals Jesus to His people. You bring the Bride into a reality of a face-to-face relationship with Jesus. The apostle is meant to do the same thing.

However, he is meant to bring a reality of the fullness of the Trinity to the Church. He helps you experience the righteous fear of the Father, the tender love and embrace of Jesus, and the fire, signs, and wonders of the Holy Spirit.

That is why your training has been what it has. You are meant to reveal to the Church the fullness of the Father, the Son, and the Spirit.

Depending on where the person you are ministering to is right now, you should be able to express the nature of God that needs to be expressed to that specific person. That is why you have gone through what you have.

That is why one minute you were trembling before the Father, the next you felt the righteousness of the Holy Spirit, and the next you felt the tender, sweet love of Jesus.

You think, "Am I going psycho? Who are you, Father?"

"I am all. I am one in three and three in one, don't you understand?"

This is part of the apostolic call. Sometimes when someone comes to us for ministry, they need Jesus, a lover and a Groom that says, "I love you. You are broken and hurt. Come and rest in my arms and let me heal you."

Then, there are times when someone needs a sign and a wonder, or a conviction of sin. Then, there are times when they need the righteousness of the Father to bring them to their knees saying, "Who are you to tell God how He should use you? He is God. He is your Father. You reverence Him."

It depends on what they need. You as an apostle should be able to reflect every aspect of the nature of God to His people, because you know God in His fullness.

I am going to end with a scripture that epitomizes that beautifully in a bit, but I want to mention the ninth function of the apostle first.

9. TO ESTABLISH A WORK THAT REMAINS (THE SEAL OF YOUR APOSTLESHIP)

Tell me, apostle, what is the seal of your apostleship?

> *1 Corinthians 9:2 If I am not an apostle to others, yet doubtless I am to you. For you are the seal of my apostleship in the Lord.*

An apostle is one who has built a structure that remains for generation after generation. Whether you are a trailblazer or builder, it does not matter. Whatever you have done should remain.

Isn't that our goal, as apostles?

You do not want to think, when all is said and done, that the winds and waves will come and wash away the work that you have done, like sand castles on a beach. You would like to imagine that you have raised up your team, imparted everything that you have, and that you have positioned them so that the work may remain.

> *2 Corinthians 2:15 For we are to God the fragrance of Christ among those who are being saved and among those who are perishing.*
>
> *16 To the one we are the aroma of death leading to death, and to the other the aroma of life leading to life. And who is sufficient for these things?*
>
> *17 For we are not, as so many, peddling the word of God; but as of sincerity, but as from God, we speak in the sight of God in Christ.*
>
> *2 Corinthians 3:1 Do we begin again to commend ourselves? Or do we need, as some others, epistles of commendation to you or letters of commendation from you?*

I am an apostle. Sorry, do I need commendation to prove to you that I am an apostle? Do I need commendation from you or even for you to say, "Yes, you are an apostle" just so that I can know who I am?

> **2 Corinthians 3:2** *You are our epistle written in our hearts, known and read by all men;*

Paul said you are our epistle, written in our hearts, known and read by all men. Do I need a degree, commendation of man, a certificate that says, "You are an apostle?" Do I even need someone to say, "I can see that you are an apostle?"

No. Let us say today, as Apostle Paul said, "You are our epistle written in our hearts, known and read by all men."

> **2 Corinthians 3:3** *Clearly you are an epistle of Christ, ministered by us, written not with ink but by the Spirit of the living God, not on tablets of stone but on tablets of flesh, that is, of the heart.*
>
> *4 And we have such trust through Christ toward God.*
>
> *5 Not that we are sufficient of ourselves to think of anything as being from ourselves, but our sufficiency is from God,*
>
> *6 who also made us sufficient as ministers of the new covenant, not of the letter but of the Spirit; for the letter kills, but the Spirit gives life.*

Apostle, when all is said and done, and you have gone through your list, confirmed your apostolic call, gotten your mandate, and are running this race, on whose heart have you written?

I do not care how many books you have under your belt, how many churches you have built, or how many ministries you have established. Tell me, who is the seal of your apostleship?

Who, not what... who is the seal of your apostleship?

What have you left in the wake of this mandate of yours? Is it just another structure of man that will be torn down again tomorrow? Or, have you birthed this mandate into those God has brought to you?

Does it matter so much to you to be called an apostle and recognized as an apostle... or simply to just BE an apostle?

I know the proof of my apostleship. It is my spiritual children, my team of mighty warriors, and those that I invest in and see rise up and do better than me.

I do not even care if I have the title. I do not care if someone says, "You think you are an apostle?"

I am like, "Really? Are we going to fight about this title?"

A title is not something you wear. It is something you do. It is something that you die for and something that you impart. If we could just allow the Spirit to bring life, instead of allowing the letter to kill, then perhaps we will start a movement.

Perhaps, we will begin something in this generation that will continue for the generations to come. It is not all about what we have done and what we have built, but who we have established and who we have raised up.

When all is said and done, one day, will I look as Christ looked when He hung on the cross and saw His inheritance?

Do you see your inheritance today? Do you look down and say, "The price is worth it because I see the inheritance in the faces of every single person that I have imparted to and raised up?"

Even if no one knows my name, I know that some fruit remains, and it is good fruit. That is why we do what we do and why we die when we die. That is why we push through when we have no more strength to push through.

It is not about me, myself, and I. The functions, mandates, and apostolic types are all very interesting and fascinating. I love to talk about it and teach about it, but you know what I love more than all of that?

I love to see the mighty warriors rise up and take their place and shake the gates of Hell and set the captives free. That is really the core of what defines us and indeed, the very reason why... we do what we do.

ABOUT THE AUTHOR

Born in Bulawayo, Zimbabwe and raised in South Africa, Colette had a zeal to serve the Lord from a young age. Coming from a long line of Christian leaders and having grown up as a pastor's kid, she is no stranger to the realities of ministry. Despite having to endure many hardships such as her parent's divorce, rejection, and poverty, she continues to follow after the Lord passionately. Overcoming these obstacles early in her life has built a foundation of compassion and desire to help others gain victory in their lives.

Since then, the Lord has led Colette, with her husband, Craig Toach, to establish *Apostolic Movement International,* a ministry to train and minister to Christian leaders all over the world, where they share all the wisdom that the Lord has given them through each and every time they chose to walk through the refining fire in their personal lives, as well as in ministry.

In addition, Colette is a fantastic cook, an amazing mom to not only her 4 natural children, but to her numerous spiritual children all over the world. Colette is also a renowned author, mentor, trainer and a woman that has great taste in shoes! The scripture to "be all things to all men" definitely applies here, and the Lord keeps adding to that list of things each and every day.

How does she do it all? Experience through every book and teaching the life of an apostle firsthand, and get the insight into how the call of God can make every aspect of your life an incredible adventure.

Read more at www.colette-toach.com

Connect with Colette Toach on Facebook!
www.facebook.com/ColetteToach

RECOMMENDATIONS BY THE AUTHOR

Note: All reference of AMI refers to Apostolic Movement International.

If you enjoyed this book, we know you will also love the following books.

THE MOSES MANDATE

Book 2 of the Apostolic Field Guide Series

By Colette Toach

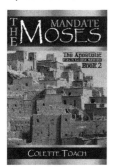

YOU, MOSES! This is your call from the wilderness. God is calling you, as an apostle, to become a Moses to lead His people out of Egypt and also create a pattern for others to follow.

God wants to give you that pattern. He wants to take you up the mountain so that you can experience His glory firsthand, and receive that pattern directly from the Father.

Colette Toach will take you through each of the apostolic types in this series, and she will show you exactly "who" God is calling you to be.

THE APOSTOLIC HANDBOOK

By Colette Toach

This book has the potential to not only confirm your calling, but launch you headfirst into the training that will take you to apostolic office.

If you have the suspicion or the strong conviction that you have been called to be an apostle, then you are on for the adventure of a lifetime. In fact, you hold in your hands a treasure map that gives you clear directions.

This book will not only tell you everything you need to know about this ministry office, but it will also TAKE YOU THERE!

DRIVING YOUR VISION FORWARD (MP3)

By Colette Toach

When Moses went into the wilderness, it was not for forever, but for a season where he had to grow and mature and where he had to become the vessel that God needed to set His people free. Once Moses was ready, God called him out of the desert.

If you desire to lead God's people out of Egypt, then it is time you receive your "burning bush" experience, and see just where exactly God wants you to lead them.

MENTORSHIP 101

By Colette Toach

Mentorship! What picture comes into your mind? It is a very hot topic in the Church today, but clear teaching is lacking. In this series, you will not only find out what the role and purpose of a mentor is, but you will see the heart that is required!

For indeed mentorship is not just about imparting knowledge, but about being a vessel for the Holy Spirit. So that He can flow through you to mold and shape your disciple. Mentorship costs a price, for both the mentor and disciple, but it is what will bring fruit that truly remains.

God is raising up His Mighty Warrior, and if you want to be on the front lines of equipping God's people, this series will show you how!

EVERYTHING IS AWESOME WHEN YOU ARE PART OF THE TEAM

By Colette Toach

Ladies and gentlemen, God has a new plan and a new idea for us - He is creating teams. He is raising up teams that can take down the enemy, teams that can stand with one another and teams that will follow through with all that He has asked of them.

The time of "God's man for the hour" is over and it has now become, "God's team for the hour". But here is the thing, He does not want just any team - He wants a team of leaders. A team that will get in there and get the job done, a team that will help lead His people out of Egypt.

Now, how does this pertain to you exactly? Well, that is what this book is here for - to help you find your team and to train you into being a part of that team.

THE MINISTER'S HANDBOOK

By Colette Toach

This is your manual on effective ministry. Whether you are dealing with an unexpected demon manifestation or you need to give marital counsel, you will find the answers here.

Colette Toach gives it to you in plain language. She gives you the steps 1, 2, 3 of how to do what God has called you to do. Keep a copy on hand, because you will come back to it time and time again!

Pastor Teacher School

www.pastorteacherschool.com

 The Lord had not called me to simply educate. He called me to train. To shape and equip His mighty warriors. I was not allowed any shortcuts. So my training never ended. To this day, He continues to shape and change me. With each lesson I learn, I pass it on to those He sends me.

This is the core of what you will find in the Pastor Teacher School - **Education by means of training**. An interactive experience that causes you to live and walk out the call that God has given to you.

Every lesson is practical, direct, and it... equips! Along with the knowledge, you gain experience and the steps to fulfilling your ministry right now.

There are many who are willing to sell you a book in the Church today, but not many who are willing to *train* you. This is what burns in us and if the Lord has sent you to our ministry, then that is what you can expect from us. A no-nonsense, boot camp that is designed to train you for your calling.

You bring your passion for God to the table and we will bring the anointing and skill to train you into what God has intended. **Together... we will change the world!**

- Colette Toach

CONTACT INFORMATION

To check out our wide selection of materials, go to: www.ami-bookshop.com

Do you have any questions about any products?

Contact us at: +1 (760) 466 - 7679
(9am to 5pm California Time, Weekdays Only)

E-mail Address: admin@ami-bookshop.com

Postal Address:

> A.M.I.
> 5663 Balboa Ave #416
> San Diego, CA 92111, USA

Facebook Page:
http://www.facebook.com/ApostolicMovementInternational

YouTube Page:
https://www.youtube.com/c/ApostolicMovementInternational

Twitter Page: https://twitter.com/apmoveint

Amazon.com Page: www.amazon.com/author/colettetoach

AMI Bookshop – It's not Just Knowledge, It's **Living Knowledge**

73562754R00152

Made in the USA
Columbia, SC
05 September 2019